# Making Conversation

## Collaborating with Colleagues for Change

### Mark Larson

*Foreword by William Ayers*

*Boynton/Cook Publishers*
HEINEMANN
Portsmouth, NH

Boynton/Cook Publishers, Inc.
A subsidiary of Reed Elsevier Inc.
361 Hanover Street
Portsmouth, NH 03801-3912

Offices and agents throughout the world.

Cataloging-in-Publication data is on file at the Library of Congress.
ISBN: 0-86709-424-9

Editor: Peter S. Stillman
Production: Renée Le Verrier
Cover design: Catherine Hawkes
Cover photo: Courtesy of the Golden Apple Foundation of Chicago
Manufacturing: Louise Richardson

Printed in the United States of America on acid-free paper.

00 99 98 97   DA   1 2 3 4 5 6

# Contents

# Contents

*To my parents,*
*who teach me to act on what I believe;*
*and Mary,*
*who artfully and lovingly guides my efforts;*
*and Emily and Sarah,*
*for whom it matters.*

*And to Susan Handler,*
*my teacher.*

*All invention and progress come from finding a link between two ideas that have never met.*

Theodore Zelden

*Where teachers are full of questions about ideas, where they talk about them—heatedly argue about them—among themselves but in range of the students, the effect is real. The kids show it. Where conditions reward both respectful candor and determined risk-taking, the self-styled curmudgeons, the respected traditionalists, the dedicated progressives, and the starry-eyed newcomers [. . .] all find the will and the reward in discovering more logical and thus more powerful ways of teaching.*

Theodore R. Sizer

*The thing about adventures, Mom, is sometimes you just have to go on 'em.*

Isaac Francis Yourist Bloom, age 8 1/2

# Acknowledgments

Unquestionably, I owe a deep debt of gratitude to my co-authors who committed their thoughts to paper and, better yet, shared them with me: Allan Alson; Raphael Altamirano; Steve Barnes; Maggie Beeler; Gretchen Burns; Laura Cooper; Kate Fiffer; Andrea Foster; Steve Gilbert; Susan Handler; Anny Heydemann; Janine N. Hill; Marvin Hoffman; Louisa Kaplan; Raquel Mathews; Clare Nelson; Dan Ring; Mary Teising-Ruggiero; Natasha Saleski; Lambert Sayles, Jr.; Liz Schaffer; Fred Schenck; Peter Seagall; Jon Seyfreid; Ari Studnitzer; Steven Terrell; Karen Van Ausdal; Rebecca Weiss. Also, my thanks to the many others whose words are not on these pages but remain with me no less. I would like to thank Allan and Laura, additionally, for being the kind of administrators who are helping make Evanston Township High School (ETHS) a place where I can, as Marv says, "explore, look stupid, fall on my face, and return to try again." I admire the courage that takes.

I would also like to acknowledge Jodie Shih-Hsieh, who managed to type portions of the manuscript from even the most illegible of handwritten notes; Emily and Sarah who typed for hours after my new laptop gulped down several huge portions of text; Mary and Sam Lawton for their many and varied contributions; Marv Hoffman and Rosellen Brown, who are new friends but already a reliable source of sustenance; Susan Aaron, who teaches teaching while she teaches piano; Becky Hodgin, Susan Young, and all my other treasured friends from Susan Handler's class who contributed so much of themselves to my education; Studs Terkel who, by his example, teaches the importance of listening to every voice; Cheryl and Bruce Roberts, who helped talk this process through; Pat and Mike Koldyke and the Golden Apple Foundation of Chicago for inspiring me with their remarkably resilient belief that, with sustained effort and hope, schools *will* serve our children better; my fellow Golden Apple fellows, especially the 95s, who never tire of talking enthusiastically and optimistically about the work we do; Paul Swanson and Rosa Sailes who don't even realize how much they contribute; my dear friend, Penny Brehman, who introduced me to Bill Ayers as well as other wonderful things; Bill Ayers, who inspires me by writing so well, working so hard, and caring so much; Steve Zemelman, who offered encouraging words early on and answered my naive questions as if they weren't; B. J. Wagner, who graciously introduced me to the larger conversation; Peter Stillman, who didn't mince words; and finally, but especially, my students, who must work overtime trying to keep me honest.

Finally, I must acknowledge the generous guidance, support, and friendship of many Evanston Township High School colleagues, most notably Virginia Ayers, Pam Baumgartner, Theresa Collins, Curt Crotty (my first and perennial teaching teacher), Cathy Donnelly, Jason Edgecombe, Naomi Feldman, Jennifer Fisher-Isquierdo, Larry Geni, Owen Hein, Janet Irons, Carol Johnson, Carol Kimmel, Syd Lieberman, Carol Lounsbury, Howard McMackin, Kathy Miehls, Val Moore, Lisa Oberman, Tom Pool, Hilda Raisner, Paula Rance, Lynn Richmond, Gene Stern, Clayton Taylor, and Warren Wolfe. Thank you for your selfless gifts.

# Foreword

*Dear Reader,*

I write to warn you about the book you're holding in your hands. Don't read it! If you've been saying recently, "I'd be a really great teacher if only I had a better batch of kids to teach," or if you regularly feel that "I'm just doing my job, and the kids are not holding up their end of the deal," or if you routinely blame the parents or society or modern times for most of the problems in your school, or if you're just barely hanging on for an imminent retirement (say, in the next fifteen to twenty years)—in short, if you've even a shred of respect for the natural order of things, "the way things have always been," and hope to maintain some small bit of peace of mind for yourself while putting in your time as a teacher, put this book down!

I'm pretty sure that Mark Larson will, in turn, delight you, infuriate you, provoke you, amuse you, and teach you. He did all that and more to me. In the dog days of his teaching, he expressed all those fearsome thoughts I detailed above. And then he scratched and clawed and wrote his way out. You might find yourself identifying with his struggle and simultaneously resisting his invitation to join. And, if you give Mark Larson half a chance, you might find in the story of his pathway toward revitalization and renewal a new, more humane way to reinvent your own teaching.

Mark Larson is no hero-teacher, no inaccessible icon, no self-help guru with a ten-step program to nirvana. He is, rather, a reflective teacher grounded in the everyday realities of classroom life. He is an idealist in the sense that he posits a standard, a goal, an inspiration to aim for in his teaching. But he is every bit a realist in the sense that he works with flesh-and-blood kids in a commonplace classroom doing the heavy lifting and the ordinary work. He writes, as it were, with one foot in a world that could be but is not yet, and the other in the mud and the muck and the green grass of this earth. In Mark Larson, the familiar tasks of teaching transcend themselves, take on a new, more satisfying shape: teaching as transformation for students and teacher alike. What is teaching, if not the invitation to change your life? And how can we invite our students, the young, to change their lives while we resolutely refuse to change our own?

The core challenges of teaching are rarely taught in colleges of education, rarely acknowledged by administrators or policymakers, and yet essential if teaching is ever to be more than clerking. Teachers must know themselves—their hopes, fears, preferences, experiences, dreams, likes, and dislikes. Teaching is intensely personal, and whatever else we teach, we teach ourselves. We are the instruments of our teaching, and knowing ourselves is essential.

Teachers must also see their students as fellow beings, as three-dimensional creatures like ourselves with a wide range of skills, interests, experiences, hopes, dreams, and intelligence that must be understood and tapped as a basis for further growth and development. The real challenge of teaching is finding human capacity (in our students, in ourselves) while working in systems that routinely highlight deficits and deficiencies. This means beginning with an assumed and unshakable faith that all students bring strengths and abilities with them into the classroom. We can then understand the key task of teaching in finding those strengths, in part by creating environments that demand and display capacity, and connecting those skills and abilities to deeper and wider ways of knowing.

For Mark Larson, writing is the vehicle to all of that. It is a way to find himself and to see his students. It is a way for everyone in his class and within his reach to unearth purpose and power and voice. The voices discovered are various: They are public voices and private voices, internal and external voices, voices of humor and conflict and anger and anguish. Musical voices. Prayerful voices. Thoughtful voices. Judgmental voices.

Mark Larson has a unique capacity to nurture and challenge colleagues and students alike in the same gesture. His remarkable honesty, his penetrating and revealing self-criticism, stand side-by-side with a brutal authenticity and a core integrity that appears unbreakable. He listens carefully to criticism, opens himself to exacting analysis and examination, while holding fast to his larger purposes and deeper goals.

Dear reader, you've come this far. Here's a book that just might change your life. Go ahead and read it.

*Best wishes,*
*William Ayers*

# Introduction

# The Continuing Conversation

*Every day's headlines show more clearly that the old ways, the "tried and true" ways, are simply and quite spectacularly not working. The time has come to do something very different. The way to begin is—to begin.*

John Holt

I won't lie to you. This book holds more questions than answers. As you may be doing right now, I have searched the bookstore shelves for that book or article that will tell me, finally, how to get my disengaged students to read or write or just show up in class. I admit it: I'm easily seduced by the hope that a book, article, or seminar exists that will address my most pressing questions and change everything. I am looking for *Ten Ideas That Never Fail for Any Student, The Only Way to Teach Literature,* and *How to Help Students Produce Dazzling Essays That Are Not Only Vivid and Full of Life but Meet District Standards, Too!* Because I am hopelessly optimistic, I never leave a bookstore empty-handed. I become convinced that this or that book is It; after all, the preface promises it will be. But though I may gain a few new insights, possibly a handful of tricks, the fact that I am back in the bookstore a week later says it all.

So I'll tell you right from the start that *Making Conversation* focuses more on what we don't know than what we do know about teaching English. But this book is propelled by the belief that by unearthing—in the full view of colleagues and students—the ques-

1

tions that keep us perennially perplexed, we are making our way toward viable, grounded answers.

Should we have a canon or should we allow students to choose the books they will read? If we have a canon, who will decide what will be in it and how will they make that decision? How do we balance student choice with our responsibility to lead children to higher ground? What does a good essay look like? How will students know when they've written it? How will we recognize it when we see it? How do we assess student progress in ways that both yield useful, reliable information and are fair to all students? How do we engage disengaged students without compromising "standards"? What *are* our standards? What is the place of "values" in our curriculum? Does "student-centered" mean I can't teach anymore?

And at the core of our discussion sits the question Peter Elbow raised in 1987: "What is English?" In other words, what is this class of ours *about*, what's *in* it, or more cynically, what's it *for*? These questions need to be raised again and again. First, because phrasing a question often prompts the process of formulating a response. Second, when we question our work openly and together, we stand a better chance of arriving at some commonality in what we believe about what needs to be taught and how we ought to teach it. But most importantly, we must develop habits of inquiry so we will be prepared for the new questions that will certainly continue to arise.

Michael Fullan calls this process of questioning and wondering *vision-building*. "Working on vision," he says, "means examining and reexamining. We should not think of vision as something only for leaders. It is not a farfetched concept. It arises by pushing ourselves to articulate what is important to us as educators." Fullan cites Block (1987), who says that articulating our vision of the future "is to come out of the closet with our doubts about the organization and the way it operates. Indeed, it forces us to come out of the closet with doubts about ourselves and what we are doing" (13).

Fullan promises that "the more one takes the risk to express personal purpose, the more kindred spirits one will find. A great deal of overlap will be experienced. Good ideas converge under the conditions of communication and collaboration" (14).

Today, I get many opportunities to talk to teachers-to-be, beginning teachers and veterans, prominent teachers and authors. And I think Fullan is right. The more I reveal about my own aspirations, apprehension, restlessness, and indecision, the more kindred spirits

I find. Today I'll gladly talk anytime with anyone about the complexities of our profession. If education wasn't my career, it surely would be my hobby.

But I didn't always feel that way. Not in the beginning. When I started my career as a teacher, I spoke infrequently with my colleagues. I stayed in my classroom and forged my own way. Other teachers were quick to offer tests, quizzes, worksheets, and advice, but we never really talked about the nature of our work, never raised questions about what we could do better. We were preoccupied with the nuts and bolts of the day-to-day operation.

In this vacuum, I developed some terrible habits. For example, I found myself behaving like the teachers I had deplored when I was a student in high school. Though I had been a recalcitrant and unsuccessful student myself, I became a rigid and uncompromising teacher. I believed it was the right thing to do. I believe now that I was acting on the only model of teaching I had ever seen. For six years, I bashed heads with my students, all the while wondering, "What's wrong with these kids?"

In 1992, I went for my masters. As part of the program, my instructor, Susan Handler, and I wrote response journals. I wrote about encounters with students, faculty, parents, and administrators. In her responses, Susan nudged me toward thinking more deeply and critically about what I did in the classroom and why I did it that way.

Now I wanted my colleagues and administrators and students to enter my thinking and to mix their thoughts with mine. I wanted to bring them into my room and be invited into theirs. Time, of course, rarely permitted frequent visits; so, as if we all lived at great distance from one another, I wrote letters. To my astonishment, I received responses.

The students were first—they always lead the way. Then I gathered my courage and sent my letters to the faculty and administration. Some teachers who did not have the time or inclination to write picked up the dialogue orally, which is fine too. Slowly but surely we are building common understandings, developing the habit of sharing, moving toward creating common goals. I like to think we are building trust and continuity—though that remains to be seen.

But I said I wouldn't lie to you. We have a long way to go. And the work is hard. Most teachers are still not part of the conversation. Some openly oppose it. Many teachers do not like to raise the questions that sometimes raise doubts about their work. Although education literature today is filled with articles about "professional growth" and collegiality, the reality is that sharing our doubts about what we do is still a difficult and risky prospect. Put bluntly, we're just not very good at it yet. Perhaps that is because we have so rarely seen it done.

*Making Conversation* does not presume to tell you how to initiate conversation in your own school, or what you should be talking about, or the answers toward which you should be moving. And I won't be confessing all the awful mistakes I've made as a teacher with the hope that you've made those mistakes too and will commiserate. Instead, *Making Conversation* offers one example of what such a conversation looked and sounded like. I've compiled here the letters and notes that passed between my students, administrators, colleagues, Susan, and me over a period of five years. These letters are our effort to write our way out of and toward the same thing simultaneously: all that we don't know.

I hope you'll see *Making Conversation* as a letter and an invitation to you.

# Chapter One

# The Beginning of the Beginning

I teach at Evanston Township High School in Evanston, Illinois, the same high school I attended in the late sixties. We have a student body of about 2,700, down considerably from the five thousand students who attended with me. Ours is the only high school in this large Chicago suburb (population: seventy-three thousand). We serve students from a variety of socioeconomic and ethnic backgrounds. There is an almost equal number of African-American and white students; each group comprises about 45 percent of the student body. Thirty-three languages are represented. We pride ourselves on our diversity.

But, as a 1995 in-house study, "ETHS Report on Minority Achievement", concluded, our school, "despite its prominence as a place which offers students a wide range of wonderful educational opportunities, fails to reach a large pool of minority students. Such students depart from the high school with skills which may be insufficient to provide them with satisfying post-high school alternatives" (1995, 1).

I was raised in a liberal household, the son of socially active parents. I can remember, for example, marching through the streets of Evanston with them for the cause of equal housing. In 1966, when I was thirteen, my father addressed the school board in an appeal for the integration of Evanston's elementary schools. But as soon as I began teaching, I found, as Herbert Kohl admits so candidly in *36 Children*, that "It's one thing to be liberal and talk, another to face something and learn that you are afraid" (1988, 13). As a beginning teacher, I was assigned four freshman classes—two low-ability (one-level) and three mid-level (two-level) groups. My one-level classes were primarily composed of African-American students. There were thirty; I had four white students. Most of the honors classes, I would later discover, were primarily white and taught by more experienced teachers. Though this situation has changed somewhat in the intervening years, a sharp disparity remains a problem while viable solutions continue to elude us.

I quickly became overwhelmed by the complexity and seriousness of the problems I faced, most of which had been absent from my own childhood: thirteen-year-olds with babies of their own, involvement with gangs, violence and the constant threat of violence, depression, substance abuse, fragmented home lives, poverty (35 percent of our students are below the poverty line), and a titanic animosity toward school. I felt wholly unprepared, by both my upbringing and my educational training, to handle the situations I faced.

At the end of my fourth year, as part of my semi-annual review process, I was asked to submit a report on my "successes in the classroom." I wrote that my successes were "painfully few" and ended the report with this story about a recalcitrant and unsuccessful student:

> Recently, Johnny, a sixteen-year-old freshman, arrived late for the fourth time that week and probably the twenty-first time this year. He said, "Guess you're gonna have to do something about it." I said I guessed I would. But I had no idea what. He sat down on the edge of my desk, brushing aside papers and books. I let him. I continued to review for the exam scheduled for the following day. Ten minutes later, Johnny raised his hand to ask a question, which pleased me. He said, "Can I get a pass home? There's catsup on my damn pants." That day, without hesitation and without a speech about his missing the test review, I gave him a pass. I have not seen him since.
>
> That moment became a turning point for me. In that moment, it became clear to me that I had done all I could for Johnny and many of the others too. My time with them would soon be over. There was probably nothing I could do that would make any difference. And now, as I write this, I grow painfully aware of how little has changed for most of my students this year.

I believe that we, as a staff, don't yet know how to address the needs nor handle the problems posed by many of our students. I've come to realize that much of my anger, fear, and sadness stems from a feeling of inadequacy in the face of all this. A friend and colleague said to me the other day that "right now, I have to say I hate what I do for a living." This year the failures so outnumber the successes that I, too, have to say I hate what I do for a living.

I'll take the summer off now. I'll return in September and, if this fall is like all other falls, I'll come back loving my job again. We'll all start over. But I won't forget that there were kids I faced this year for whom we did precious little.

The supposedly inarticulate can often be pointedly cogent when we bother to listen. Johnny offered us a challenge on the last day I saw him: "You're gonna have to do something."

Respectfully submitted,
Mark Larson

An administrator responded to my report by suggesting I "might be happier in a different school, or perhaps even in some other career." End of conversation.

I spent the next several years searching on my own for ways to be responsive to the needs of my students. For much of that time I was a tyrant, believing that what my kids needed most was what appeared to me to be lacking from their lives: order. I made order my mission. I struggled to maintain it in both my classroom and the halls. My assignments were precisely prescribed, even to the point where I was telling students how many sentences long a paragraph should be. I forced them to number each sentence and checked to be sure they correlated with the numbered sentences in the "model" essay I gave them, a dreary piece of my own writing about my three favorite possessions. Sentence Number 1: topic sentence; Sentence Number 2: follow-up; Sentence Number 3: first reason or example to support main idea.

I found myself increasingly intolerant of anything that did not fit my rigid idea of order, both within and outside of my classroom. The hallways of ETHS, which were then often loud and chaotic, became my battlefield. I tell you with no small amount of shame that I was known to chase after those students I considered malefactors. I was called a racist by some, a bleeding heart by others; I was neither. But

I took both accusations seriously and found my head spinning. At one point, I was blacklisted by a member of the community who had compiled a list of twenty teachers who needed to be "watched." I was furious and frightened at the time. Now I think I did need to be watched. I was out of control. I was a do-gooder doing no good.

At the height of my bewilderment, Studs Terkel interviewed me about my experiences for his book, *Race: How Blacks and Whites Think and Feel About the American Obsession.* Halfway through our conversation, as he fumbled to change tapes, he told me he thought it would be better if he did not publish my real name. He created the pseudonym, Peter Soderstrom, so I could retain my Swedish heritage without risking my actual identity. I wondered what I was saying that would warrant such a precaution? I read it today and I know I was lost, confused. But the most positive aspect of the experience is that it got me to reflect, for the first time, on what was happening to me, to ask questions of myself. Studs and I sat on a couch in his living room and talked for almost four hours.

He had begun by asking me, "Who are you?"

> I'm a teacher, trying to do the right thing. It's becoming more and more difficult [. . .] I get mad, but the Swede in me tries to control it and lets me know it's not constructive. Yet [the kids and I] end up yelling at each other. I am an adult, I'm a teacher. I say: "You can't talk to me that way." It's funny when I say it now, because I've said it so many times. I just feel so appalled. And humiliated, too. Really humiliated. I need to deal with that with myself. I've been told to back off because I'm going to have trouble. I know some kids have threatened me. I know I've caused trouble because I'm being confrontational. My last period of the day is free, so I leave before three though I'm supposed to stay until four. I leave because I know I'm not going to deal well with it. A friend said, "It's like watching someone burn out."
>
> This year has really made me look at myself to see what is going on. What word am I looking for? To reevaluate. Am I becoming a racist? Of my new batch of kids, two-thirds will be black. I know exactly what [they'll be like]. Am I prejudging? Prejudiced? What's happening to me? (1992, 194)

It was about this time that I started graduate school at National

Louis University. Dr. Susan Handler, my teacher, asked us to submit weekly journals in which we described or discussed encounters—either with individuals or groups. This is one of my first submissions:

One-level teachers never meet together. A couple of years ago, I told an administrator that if a committee was ever formed to search for solutions and strategies for working with one-level kids, I'd be interested. He replied, "I know of no such group." And the conversation was closed—for two years.

Last year, I decided to form a committee myself to see what would happen. My friend, Lisa Oberman, and I put a notice in the daily bulletin inviting all one-level teachers to begin a conversation about the common problems we all face.

I was worried about how the administration would react to this. A year ago, Lisa and I had submitted a letter to the school board that described in pretty graphic detail the belligerent behaviors we had witnessed among ETHS students. We held all adults, from community members to faculty and the board, responsible, anyone who was in a position to act but had failed to do so. By the time Lisa read the letter to the board, it had been signed by 144 teachers. A few committees were later formed to examine the problem and offer solutions. I was ready and eager to work within the system. But, to my surprise, I was not asked to serve on any committee in any capacity.

I went to the superintendent and pleaded with him to include me. I told him that when I wrote the letter I felt, for the first time, that I was not powerless. I also felt less isolated because I had begun receiving notes from teachers who wanted to tell me their own stories. He said flatly that the committees were full. When I persisted, he said he'd look into it, see what he could do. I never heard from him again on this matter.

So as I prepared my classroom for the one-level meeting, I kept wondering how the administration would react to it. I nervously arranged a circle of nine desks and waited. Two, then five, then seven persons arrived. One of those persons was an administrator who did not return my greeting and would sit in stony silence throughout the meeting. By four o'clock, we had to widen our circle to include twenty-two desks. We talked for almost two hours.

I had caught a glimpse of what can happen when teachers share not just quizzes and worksheets, but also doubts and fears—and dreams and ideas.

Until I talked to Studs Terkel and later, when his book came out, to teachers who read the chapter and told me they felt the same helplessness I described, I had worked in almost complete isolation. Today I believe that I started to become a different teacher the moment he leaned toward me and asked that disarmingly simple question, "Who are you?" It led me to ask myself what I still consider a chilling question, "What's happening to me?" The desire to search for answers grew stronger every day.

## Books I Wish I'd Known About at the Time

*To Teach: The Journey of a Teacher*, William Ayers.
*City Kids, City Teachers*, William Ayers.
*Other People's Children*, Lisa Delpit.
*36 Children*, Herbert Kohl.
*Teaching English So It Matters*, Deborah Stern.
*I Won't Learn From You*, Herbert Kohl.

# Chapter Two

# Discoveries: Deciding to Change

*We must try harder to understand than to explain.*
Vaclav Havel

When my students are stuck in their writing or unable to begin, I give them the same advice John Holt offers teachers in *What Do I Do Monday?* I tell them that the only way to begin—is to begin. Irritatingly simplistic advice, I know. If they knew how to begin, they say, they *would* begin. Fair enough. So I break the beginning down for them. I ask them, "What do you want to say in this essay? What do you want to accomplish?" Or, "How do you want this to sound: serious, comic, what?" If they can't start at all, I ask them what they think stands in their way. Or we just talk—about their day, their week, their life—until they hit on something that makes their eyes light up. Then I say, "Why don't you write about that?" Often I find that they are stuck because they are expecting the essay or story to arrive full-blown, like Athena from the head of Zeus. They are either too impatient to start with what they have (the mere seed of an idea) or they don't recognize what they have as a seed, tightly packed with potential.

Perhaps you sometimes feel this way as a teacher. You want to begin something new, but are unable to take the first step. Maybe you are dissatisfied with some aspect of your teaching, or you have a growing desire to change everything, as I did. But how and where to start? The task seems daunting, the path ahead uncertain. If you're like my students and me, you may want to get it right on the first shot. I didn't even realize my own tendency to think this way until a teacher wrote to me a few years ago and said she was getting ready to implement portfolios in her class. "Is it OK," Theresa asked, "for me to be in process on this as I go, or should I have something polished before I begin?" I suggested that she not wait. "Nothing," I realized, "will be polished until it rubs against the kids."

There's a wonderful line about this in Tony Kushner's *Angels in America*. One of the characters, Harper, articulates what the audience, with her help, has come to understand: "You need an idea of the world to go out into the world," she says. "But it is the going into that makes the idea. You can't wait for a theory, but you have to have a theory" (147). This seeming paradox sits at the center of our discussion of personal change. We need an idea, a theory, yes, but part of the nature of that theory is that it will be formed by the "going into" our work. The *going into* requires a leap of faith, of course, but it has potential for creating a constructive friction between being and becoming. With any luck, in time we will find we are in motion.

Just begin, says John Holt. And I add: The beginning of the beginning is a question.

Studs Terkel helped me find a starting place when he asked me who I was, then sat back to listen. "I am a teacher," I said, "trying to do the right thing." With that declaration, my interest shifted from creating order at all costs to discovering what, as an English teacher, I should be doing and how I should be doing it. What, as an English teacher, *is* the right thing? I quickly learned that there are no road maps to the answers. As Myles Horton says, we make the road by walking. But I was lucky. I learned to find my way in Susan Handler's Master's of Education program at National Louis University in Evanston, Illinois.

Every Monday evening, for two years, I joined eighteen women and one other man at a large round table in Susan's classroom. She often opened sessions by asking us what we had "brought to the table." We brought our victories and defeats, disappointments, doubts, fears, and questions. Night after night, she managed to render whatever we brought to the table into the stuff of the curriculum for that evening's session. I owe a lot to Susan. She taught me to listen by listening, to care by caring, to question by questioning. In short, she taught me to teach by example—in both senses of that phrase. She taught by her own example and, in so doing, taught me the power of modeling. She was genuinely interested in us as teachers, as students, as people, and in the light of her interest, we would unfold.

What interested me most about my relationship to this class was my resistance to it. As if two decades hadn't passed since I was a recalcitrant high school student myself, I picked up where I left off—refusing to do my homework. During the entire two years of the program, I don't think I read more than five of the assigned works.

Although Susan would later admit that she often bristled whenever I proclaimed to the class that I was unprepared, she did not criticize this resistance. She watched it, curious; it is what I brought to the table. Her curiosity, coupled with the freedom she gave me not to read, provided me time and a deepening desire to come to understand my own obstinancy, if indeed that's what it was. Most importantly, however, she got me to think about and articulate my resistance. I was coming to learn about who I was as a student. This, in turn, led to discoveries about teaching and learning that would change my career. I gained a fuller, more complex understanding, not only of my own academic character, but also that of many of my students—students like Sheldon, for example.

On the first day of school, Sheldon called me a jag-off. Before the first week had passed, he was suspended for physically threatening another teacher. "Tellin' you, watch your back. Gonna take you down." His counselors recommended a battery of psychological tests. We actually had begun to wonder if Sheldon could read and write at all. He was doing neither. He was failing several classes and frequently getting into severe trouble with the dean for acting up in class. He had several lengthy suspensions for a variety of infractions. The first essay he turned in was two pages long: his own name repeated probably five hundred times. He entitled it "Sheldon."

But I liked Sheldon. I was intrigued by what he was bringing to the table: resistance. I wondered what would happen if I met him on his ground, rather than punish him for not meeting me on mine. I accepted his "essay" for inclusion in his writing file, something I never would have done in the past. I didn't say it was good writing, I simply said, "Let's not lose this." I felt like I had been duped, which, of course, I had. But I tried to place myself, my own feeling of being the fool, in the background, as Susan had done with me, and see if Sheldon would emerge. That was neither as simple nor as easy as it may sound. I still found it difficult not to feel personally violated by a student's behavior, whether it took the form of resistance, rejection, or withdrawal. But I tried to keep in mind something Susan had once written to me:

> As a teacher, I think it is important not to rage against another's resistance. Much anxiety is stirred up in us when our students don't do their (our) work: "He's lazy! She's manipulative! They don't care!" But this is our injury we are suffering. As the rage increases on both sides, the kid is lost.

In this sense, I know I had "lost" many, many students. Now I wanted to discover Sheldon. After I put the "Sheldon" essay in his file, I asked him what he planned to write next. He shrugged. I offered a few ideas, then waited for more writing. Anxiously. Nothing happened. Metamorphosis can be exasperatingly slow. Theirs and mine.

Then one day he came into the computer lab, sullen and angry, his usual mood. This day, however, I asked him what was going on.

"This is the worst day of my life."

"What happened?"

"*Nothing.* It's just the worst day of my life, *OK?*"

I slipped his disk into the computer and called up a blank screen. I typed the words, "This is the worst day of my life," and turned to walk away.

He stopped me. "I can write about that?"

"Sure," I said.

Sheldon, whose ability to even write at all the counselors and I had questioned, wrote an essay, which began:

> Today is the worst day of my life. I think ETHS is the worst high school in all of Chicago land. I don't like most of the teachers and I hate [the dean]. I also don't like most of the kids in the school and I hate the food in the cafeteria. I don't know what's wrong this year, but it seems like whatever I do is wrong. I have all ready gotten three inside suspensions, about fifteen referrals, and about fifty detentions. I want to change all my classes and start over again.

Something important was initiated at that moment, for him and for me. If he would write words that honestly—"I don't know what's going wrong. . . . I want to start over"—what else might he write?

And where were all the serious writing "problems" we anticipated? And why had we interpreted resistance as inability? And most unsettling, how many times in the past had I made this same error in judgment?

Now I wondered what would happen if I let all my students write on any topic they wanted or needed to write on. What if I searched for ways to help them discover what was most pressing to them at that moment, then helped them articulate it in writing? What if I worked with whatever they brought to the table? If they were more invested in their writing, would my comments about basic skills fall on more attentive ears? Was it possible that a reason they had always written such bland prose, when they wrote at all, was because I had been asking them to write *my* essays, the essays I had in mind, instead of what was on their mind? If that was true, no wonder they didn't care about spelling and punctuation. The piece didn't even belong to them. Maybe that's why they frequently left all those "careless errors" for me to correct, as if I were their proofreader instead of their writing teacher.

Reflexively, I feared that without my giving them a topic and a rigid format for their essays, they would write junk and never learn skills they'd need in the work force. But the argument I had once held fast—that they must learn to write functional essays, business letters, and memos if they were going to survive in the big world — began to unravel when I asked myself whether I really wanted to make a career of teaching students to write bland, ordinary prose. Wasn't it possible that as they gained confidence in their writing, they could write whatever they wanted to write, including memos?

In the coming months, Sheldon wrote six more essays, most of them two to three pages in length. All of them were about his troubles with school or his girlfriend.

> When I got to her house, just five minutes after we talked on the phone, there she was with the ape man Derrick. That's why I had to do him that way and yeah, I'm sorry about his tooth and how he had to get stitches. But right is right. And he wasn't no way right. But the truth is me sticking him with that barBQ fork wasn't no way right neither. So square one I got to make some changes about me. Faster in fast.

I would return the essays and tell him what the piece made me think about and feel as a reader. I didn't mark any mechanical errors at that point. I was determined to build on what he gave me rather than chip away at it. Later, I could focus on skills, when he was ready to polish the piece, when the thing was absolutely his. First, I wanted to help him see his writing as a means of communication rather than as a school task to grudgingly complete to avoid punishment.

By the end of the first semester, he was handing me essays and demanding that I read them immediately. "Peek this quick," he'd say, dropping his latest in my lap and falling into a chair next to mine. One time, I was extremely busy and when he demanded that I peek his essay, I said, "I can't now, Sheldon. I don't have time." Quarterly reports were due. I'd hoped to use the computer lab time to finish mine. But Sheldon persisted and I relented. It wouldn't be the first time my reports were late. His essay was about how he "had to fight this guy today"; how he "had to do what he had to do." I told him that *I* had to report my knowledge of this fight. He stood quickly, knocking over his chair. "Man, that's not even right! I thought you was cool. You a fake, man, no lie. Why you wanna be a chump and tell for?"

"I don't want anything to happen to you," I said.

To my utter amazement, Sheldon's eyes, usually hard and intense, blurred with tears. There was no fight, at least not on that day.

Once I started listening, the way Susan had listened to me, I learned something important, both about my students and about me. The spring before Sheldon's class came to me as freshmen, they had suffered an intolerable loss. One of their thirteen-year-old classmates, Marchelle, had been shot and killed by a kid not much older than herself. Many students had written about Marchelle but, as strange as it may seem in retrospect, the message that an actual person, a friend of theirs, had been brutally killed, escaped my notice. At least its importance didn't sink in. I had been that focused on their getting the writing format correct.

> There are three main reasons why I will miss Marchelle. The first reason is. . .

With that humbling realization, I knew I was ready to take another small step. I gave Sheldon's class (just one of my five classes) the same opportunity I had given Sheldon. I told them that for their next assignment they could "write what you care about" and in any way they wanted to write it. I figured that even if they turned in a three-sentence essay that they had written in the hallway moments before the bell, one wasted assignment wouldn't hurt. It now seemed worth the risk.

The results surprised me. I received an essay from Malik about the day, just a month earlier, when his father fell dead of a heart attack before his own eyes.

> At first I thought he was joking, falling down like that. He used to joke a lot, probably too much as says my mom. But he hit the driveway hard that's how I knew. Still in his pajamas my dad was dead.

There's something haunting about the phrasing of the line: "Still in his pajamas my dad was dead." I could not have taught that. But could I, as a teacher, work toward creating a place where a phrase like that could happen?

Kesha, an African-American student, wrote about her spring-break trip to Mississippi during which she came face to face with raw prejudice for the first time.

> The people in [the fast-food restaurant] were really rude for starters. They threw our bags and food at us and said we can bag it ourself. But when we sat down is when it got really bad. A guy in the corner by himself pointed his finger at us shaped like a gun. Each one of us, he quote-unquote "shot" one at a time. I always heard about prejudice but never had to see it in somebody's face up close like that. I was too sad to be mad.

Many students turned their attention back to Marchelle.

> We shared our life for thirteen years,
> We shared our smiles and our tears,
> From kindergarden to junior high,
> We were happy together you and I.
> You made me mad on the ninth of May
> I was waiting on you forever that day.
> I called and I called, but you weren't home.

The streets is where you decided to rome.
Why didn't you do as you were told?
Just left me in the cold.
Then that next morning which was Mother's Day,
I heard that a grave was where you'd lay.
I'm glad you're in Heaven not in Hell
I just want you to know that I love you Marchelle.

Is it great writing? No. Does it need work? A lot. But finally I had something I never had before: interest, enthusiasm, a starting place.

I sent samples of the kids' work to Susan and told her what I had tried. She wrote back:

> I was pleased to see that you were doing things differently. Isn't it amazing the response you are getting when you say, "Write what you want to write"? It seems to unlock some of them. Kids who had done nothing for your class all year suddenly produce work. Instead of saying, "No, I am not going to do the piece you want me to do," they seem to shift when they are given the opportunity to design some of the parameters of the task, when their own "person" is seen. I don't think this is magic; I think it is a human response to the longing we all feel to be considered, to be asked—not demanded—to give.
>
> Their lives are emergencies. I don't see how their needs, their suffering, their fears could be locked out of your English curriculum. I feel you are knocking down some of the walls between inside and outside of school for them and inviting free flow between the two. I think it is essential.
>
> Let me know how it continues.

After I received that batch of essays, eight weeks remained before the end of the year. I didn't want to lose what I perceived to be a gathering momentum. I thought I'd take another small step. I had heard about "portfolios," but didn't really understand how they worked. At that time I had been doing very little reading of professional literature. So I operated on a general and uninformed notion that a portfolio was just a collection of student writing. That was a place to start. Later, when my interest was piqued, and I had a context into which I could place new information, I would find my way to the plethora of books and articles on portfolios and portfolio assessment.

My crude version of portfolios was this: I would ask students (again, in just that one class) to write three essays for their portfolio (actually a manila folder) over the course of the final quarter. The essays could be written on any topic they chose. Students could turn their writing in when they were ready for me to see it. They attached a cover sheet (Appendix A) and in the margins they asked me questions: "Is the part about the fight scary or just stupid?"

I would read the papers, answer the questions, make suggestions, then return them to be rewritten (Appendix B). I told my students I would not put a grade on any writing. It seemed an inadequate response. We would work toward "completion". Once the student and I agreed that a piece of writing was finished, I would hit it with a rubber stamp: COMPLETED. (Incidentally, in answer to the question I often heard from my colleagues: No, I got very little resistance from students or parents. Eliminating grades on papers was not nearly the cataclysmic event we sometimes anticipate, as if grades were the screws that hold the huge educational machine together. They aren't. In fact, I saw students work much harder for "completion" than they ever had worked for a grade.)

But what constitutes a "completed" essay? Good question, the answer to which continues to elude me. I know it's not enough to say, "We'll know it when we see it." And yet, when talking about writing, there may be some legitimacy to that proposition as a "standard."

A major publishing house once wrote to my agent about my perennially unpublished novel. She said that I had tackled a large topic "with strength and sensitivity" and that the book had "considerable merits in terms of style and subject." In fact, she said, "I've gone back and forth on this one." But, ultimately, it "just didn't quite work for me. I'm sorry I can't be less vague about my complaint but really, it's a very strong book." Huh?

I understand the importance of specific standards in schools, but maybe there are ways to reconcile that requirement with the hard-to-pin-down nature of good writing. The standard will necessarily vary as the writer switches her attention from one audience to another, or tries to achieve various purposes. When we try to be very specific about writing standards, considerations such as taste, style, vitality, and originality seem to fly out the window. At my school, at least, we eliminate the problem of vague concepts by demanding rigidly formatted writing: *topic sentence, three supports, and a conclusion.* One can know, even without really reading, whether a student has written "well" or not. But I have worked with too many upperclassmen who cannot break themselves of opening every essay with "There are many reasons why. . . ." and ending with "These are just some of the reasons why. . . ." This is not writing, it's xeroxing.

In response to the uproar in the national press that followed the publication of NCTE's Standards for English, Jim Burke defended the document's supposed vagueness, saying that "What is vague challenges us as nothing else can. [The standards] do not offer precise, delineated steps some would expect. What they offer is much more important: a framework for meaningful discussion about how best to teach English" (*Education Week*, 4/3/96). In a similar way, my lack of specificity about what constituted a completed essay (though admittedly the result of a lack of planning on my part) gave rise in the grade conferences to some fascinating discussions about writing in general and the student's own writing in particular. I think these discussions yielded powerful lessons for the students and for me as we struggled to articulate why this or that piece worked or didn't work.

I must sound like I'm advocating vagueness, hardly a cause that would garner wide public support. "Stand up for vagueness!" But I'm not advocating it as much as coming to a realization that we could be working with fuzzy concepts (good writing, good books, values) and trying to find ways to come to grips with that. The problem of how to define specific, reliable standards, especially for writing, would remain on the table for me. (See Chapter 6: Assessment.)

I was very happy with some of the writing our experimentation with portfolio assessment yielded. I learned that there is something very potent about giving students a say in what they will write about and how they will present it. The kids were able to respond immediately in writing to problems or triumphs they were facing.

For example, during this time, Lachisa, a junior, was attending the trial of the young man who murdered her cousin. When she wrote for my class, she recounted the events of the trial, the arguments that arose between her family and the killer's family, the callousness of both attorneys. Writing seemed to help her sort out her mix of confusing emotions. I would have hated to have to say, "That's interesting, Lachisa, but we're working on business letters now."

Working without a specific schedule or standard had many drawbacks, too, however. There were kids who whipped off those easy, five-minute poems and stuck them in their files, having learned nothing about writing. "There, I'm done!" And since I set no due dates, except for a final day by which all work had to be completed, many students waited until the last minute, sending me home with a milk crate full of papers. So while I was pleased with the work most students produced, there remained some difficult problems to be worked out and questions to be answered. I was not comfortable with the looseness of the course. I felt there had to be a structure within which this looseness operated.

At the end of one year, I wrote to Susan about a group of students who, over the course of the year, had grown increasingly out of control. I had realized, too late, that they needed more structure and guidelines than I was giving them, but at the time I didn't know how to provide that structure and balance it with the freedom that had nonetheless produced some interesting results in the areas of student engagement and experimentation, in both their writing and reading choices. Susan responded that she was working with a master's class of adults with which she faced the same dilemma. However, says Susan,

> the adult version of being out of control was not to engage themselves—in reading, ideas, conversation. My hunch now is that I expected too much of them. I expected them to make use of the freedom I gave them to find their own curiosity and interest. I think they needed more help than I gave them.
>
> Kids (adults) need guidance in how they organize the tasks we give them, in how they assess their reactions, in how they proceed when they feel frustrated or ashamed with not knowing. It is always a sublime pleasure when groups of students take off with your invitation. It feels as though they have been waiting for someone to ask them what they feel and think. They welcome the request with delight and relief. And others, I think, are baffled and upset. They truly need more guidance to engage themselves in the process because they don't know how. We need to fill in some of the blanks through a series of activities or experiences that move them from place to place. We can't rightfully expect them to leap. They don't have the trust in their abilities to leap; perhaps they feel it is far too dangerous. I think William Glasser is incomplete. He doesn't talk about the interventions, both curricular and interpersonal, that the teacher needs to make to move the group toward "quality work."

Now I had unraveled many of my old assumptions about teaching and learning, about what makes writing "good" and what motivates students. But the more I unraveled, the more questions I seemed to face. And, with what was I left? A course hindered by a bewildering and unsettling lack of coherence and precision.

## Books I Wish I'd Known About at the Time

*Clearing the Way*, Tom Romano
*In the Middle*, Nancie Atwell
*Writing Your Way*, Peter Stillman
*Writing with Power*, Peter Elbow
*A Fresh Look at Writing*, Donald Graves

# Chapter Three

# Transition: Making a Change

*Even in the face of wracking doubts about the possibilities for change, we must act as if change is within reach, lest our children inherit from us a paralyzing pessimism and resignation that ensure that no change will occur. Against tremendous obstacles, it is up to us to, at the very least, emulate the heartening resilience of so many of our courageous students.*

Marvin Hoffman

Next came an awkward period of transition, a kind of career adolescence, replete with exaggerated mood swings, a recurrent identity crisis, and a spirit of recklessness. Once I had "discovered" the potential of student empowerment, I let kids voice their opinion on everything from our class schedule to how we would handle the bathroom pass. "How many trips, do *you* think, is too many trips?" Entire class periods could be spent discussing what would happen next—which, of course, became what happened next.

By this time, all of my classes were using portfolios. I gave no grades on any assignment. Students worked on papers until they were "completed," though I still could not have told you what constituted a completed paper. And I set no due dates. The kids turned work in when they were ready for me to see it. On top of that, I wanted to understand every kid, wanted to hear the story behind their behavior: "*Alex, is there a special reason you slammed Arnie's face into his desk?*"

Then it hit the fan. The kids had had enough. I wrote to Susan:

Help! Last Thursday, one of my classes broke into a diatribe about how boring *To Kill A Mockingbird* is, how twenty pages is too much for me to expect them to read in one night—"WE GOT OTHER CLASSES TOO, Y' KNOW!"—how we never read anything good, like Stephen King. I listened. And listened. And the more I listened, the more freely they threw those verbal tomatoes. I tried to respond fairly, acknowledge their complaints and concerns, but also tried to explain that there are certain parameters within which we must work. If we were, for example, to read five pages a night, as someone suggested, we would still be reading this book come summer.

The discussion got under my skin. (And I'd thought I was beyond that!) I have always loved doing this book. In the past, the kids have loved it too. I did it earlier than usual this year because *Romeo and Juliet* had gone poorly and *Mockingbird* was one of my sure-shots. I was also frustrated because, for the most part, the more vocal students were the ones who showed no evidence of having read the book at all. I wanted to mention that, but worried about the kids who may be making the effort to read, but struggling. I didn't want them to think I was accusing them of not reading.

The class rejected every compromise I offered. I was being unfair, a tyrant, a *teacher* thinking more highly of the book than of them. I didn't really want to hear their point of view, they said. I was just a phony.

And then: "I think maybe you want to fail us!"

That hit hard. I looked directly at Shante who had delivered the blow and said, "I try so hard to—"

I didn't get the sentence out. Shante mimicked my words, added a pout, and pretended to cry. The kids howled. Order was demolished. I raised my hands in surrender and said, "I can't deal with you right now." I glanced at the clock. One minute remained in the period. I walked straight into the office that adjoins my room, and slammed the door shut.

Uproar. A mix of hilarity and indignation. "What's his problem? What's he doing? He's crying!"

Through the narrow window in the door, I saw a half-dozen faces peering at me. I picked up a book and pretended to read. Then the bell rang and I could hear them leave, taking their raucous news—"We made Larson cry!"—into the hall with them.

The second bell rang and the halls cleared. I set the book

down and stared at my shoes for a long time. Finally, I got up and opened the door. Loletia stood before me. Terrific. She had been angry with me for a week because I had given this journal entry to a social worker:

**Why I Don't want to Be on this earth No More.**

I hating being on this earth anymore. I have no purpose in living. It is very unfair. I have thought of many times taking my life. Everybuddy they wants to complain about my aditude. but no one ever ask me why i have this aditude or why I am frowning.

She stared at me, seemed to be searching my face for something, tears maybe. Was she glad to see me hurt? I smiled, "Aren't you going to be late?"

She said, "Don't you be gettin' crazy on us too."

The next day I stood at the door and greeted my students one at a time, as I always do. When the bell rang, I closed the door slowly. I still hadn't decided whether I would comment on what had happened the day before or pretend it had never occurred. Once they were all seated, Marcus decided for me.

"Why you always mad at us for?"

The room got quiet. Some kids put their heads down, one even covered his ears, embarrassed, I imagine, at the prospect of personal disclosure. I told them I *do* like to hear what they have to say. But I am a human, too, I said, and sometimes enough is enough.

"You slammed the door!" Loletia said. That seemed to be what bothered her most, so I apologized.

Marcus said, "Everybody be sayin' you was cryin'."

I told him that I cried when my grandparents died, when my children were born, and when a student I cared about was arrested on a serious charge. I did not cry because my second-period class got out of control.

They laughed at that. Even Loletia smiled. And we moved on. For this moment, in this room, stability was restored. It all makes me wonder how much they count on my equilibrium.

Susan responded:

First let me say I believe these students care about you a great deal—as much as you care about them—despite their current behavior. Under their assault on you, lies themselves—struggling readers.

There must be reciprocity in the room between you and them. As much as you are there to take care of them, they have an obligation not to cross a line; that line has to do with humiliating you, complaining beyond reasonable limits, hurting your feelings. Since you treat them fairly, they must reciprocate.

Communicate to them in everything you say and do that you are trying to find ways to make reading satisfying. They have, I believe, responsibility in helping you do this.

Until I heard from Susan, I had lost sight of my students' obligations to me. In the past, that's all I thought about. "You don't do my work. You cut my class. You don't show me respect." Then I swung the other way. "What can I do for you? Tell me what you need. I want to understand you." But now I needed to remind myself that I was still the teacher; I had, presumably, something to offer that they could not get from one another, and not from themselves. So I was back to Studs Terkel's question, which I had since elaborated to, "Who am I in the classroom?" I think that when I first started teaching I could have answered that question fairly easily. I might have said, "I am the decider, the dispenser, the expert, the cop, the judge, the star". But now the definition was becoming more complex and ambiguous.

I have a colleague who, every time the words "student-centered" come up in conversation, throws up her arms and says, "But we're *teachers*," as if there is a universal definition of that word, or that student-centered means all we do is stand by and watch whatever it is the kids decide to do. Of course that is inaccurate, but I understand the essence of her complaint. We are hired to be in a classroom because we know something our students don't, we have something to offer. Stating exactly what that something was, however, only grew more puzzling the more I thought about it.

As I struggled to discover and articulate what was at the core of my class, I made many blunders. And the kids always found ways to let me know they were uncomfortable with my exploration. Here is a letter I wrote to my Advanced Placement class after a discussion of *As I Lay Dying*. They had become frustrated because the discussion didn't "go anywhere." They seemed to want our talks to lead ultimately to an answer. I think they wanted to check their own answers against the "correct" answer. They didn't like the idea of simply exploring their own responses to the book, and I still wasn't very good at helping guide that exploration.

One day, as part of our preparation for the AP test, we had tried to come up with some sort of statement of theme that we all could agree upon. The conversation, I thought, had taken many interesting turns. Then five minutes before the final bell, I tried to summarize what we had discussed. I told them how pleased I was to find that we might be getting close to a workable statement. One girl, Stephanie, looked at the clock and rolled her eyes. The period was almost over and apparently she did not want to go home empty-handed.

"Just *tell* us!" she pleaded, and the class applauded.

So that night I wrote this letter and read it to them the next day. It was the first of many letters I would write to my students.

"Just tell us," you cry in frustration. You want to know the theme, what the author had in mind. "Just tell us!" I understand your frustration and am sympathetic. I have felt and continue to feel it myself, both as a teacher and as a reader. But at the risk of frustrating you further, I have to respond, "Tell you what?" Tell you what the author had in mind? I suspect that if the author was determined for you to get his theme exactly, he would have printed it upside down at the bottom of the page— that, or he would have overwritten. Tell you what the critics say? Which critic or critics? The ones I select? Or are we assuming that all critics are saying basically the same thing? Anyway, if you want to know what the critics have to say, walk down to the library. Just to the left of the front door are shelves full of literary criticism. I can't imagine you want me to do your legwork for you.

Yesterday, I asked you to try to articulate what you thought might be a theme of Faulkner's book. I'd like to encourage you now to think about how you react when you are asked to perform a task, such as stating a theme, writing a paper, or whatever. Often, the first thing we face is a void. "What will I write about? What do I think of this book? What's the answer he has in mind? Where do I begin?"

How do you react? Maybe you feel exhilaration. Some people like voids. Or maybe you feel frustration, anger, hopelessness. Panic!

Pretend this is true: what you are feeling when you face the yawning void is creative energy, the same energy you feel at the start of any creative enterprise. You are looking at the blank page, the lump of clay, the empty stage—the void. The beauty and the responsibility of that moment is that *anything is possible*. When we feel secure with our abilities, that energy can be immediately channeled in a productive direction. When we feel insecure, that energy can start to metamorphose into other things: frustration, anger, hopelessness. "This is a dumb assignment! I hate this book! I'll never be able to do this! Just tell us!"

I'm recommending that when you get that tight feeling in your chest, try to harness it and begin to build. Start with what you have. And trust yourself, trust your own intellectual capacity. Recently, one of my two-level juniors read a true story about an African-American boy his own age who lives in a world of poverty and violence. In response to the question, "What did this reading make you realize?", he responded: "I guess I realized that in the violent, weird, and totally chaotic world Nicholas [the character] lives in, people have to figure out that they really need each other."

I found this to be a clear, if not touching, and perfectly apt statement of theme. After almost a decade of experience with well over a thousand students, I could pretty well guarantee that if I had asked him what the theme of this story was he would have clammed up. Either that or he would have fumbled around with something he thought I expected to hear.

I have come to think that we may lack not the ability to understand what we read or to articulate what we think of it, but confidence in our ability to do that. Remember the responses I got when I asked you to write down what you thought was a central idea in *Waiting for Godot*? One of you said, "To me it's about friendship, but I know it has to be something more." Someone else said, "I don't think I got it right." And from many of you I heard the cry, "You're not going to read these out loud, are you?"

Here's something Emerson said in "Self-reliance." I'd be interested in your reaction.

A man should learn to detect and watch that gleam of

light which flashes across his mind from within, more than the luster of the firmament of bards and sages. Yet, he dismisses without notice his thought, because it is his. In every work of genius, we recognize our own rejected thoughts: they come back to us with a certain alienated majesty" (1983, 259).

I invite written rebuttals.

At the end of the day one student, Colleen, left the following hastily (and angrily) written note on my desk.

Finally! I have transcended English class! I don't need my classmates, or teachers or the critics. I don't have to listen to anyone else's voice. And why bother? They're not making sense, anyway!

I will go home and when I sit down to write I will figure everything out. The mysteries of literature will all become clear. And the ones that don't—well, they must not be important because I now know I don't need a teacher to learn! Who cares about classes! Who cares about symbolism and imagery and metaphor! If I can't figure them out on my own, they can't be of much use. For after all, who knows better than I do what I need to learn and to know?

So get the teacher out of here! I don't need anyone but me! I am self-motivated, self-directed, I am the best teacher I can have!

I responded to Colleen the next day:

I understand that you were being sarcastic, but I'd like to respond to your words at face value rather than to the frustration that gave rise to all those exclamation points. You make some very interesting points and criticisms that deserve a response.

I disagree. We do need to hear each other's voices until they do make sense. We don't give up hope on that. Not after nine months or four years or ten years. I'm forty-two and a long way from giving up hope that the next words I hear might tilt me, even slightly, on my axis and give me a new view of the same universe.

I disagree. You don't have the only valid idea of what you need to learn. You have—or will have—the most valid idea. But in order for you to shape and understand that notion, you need room to feel your own way in the dark, while remaining in the relative safety of a learning environment—er, pardon the jargon, I meant classroom.

Finally, I hope you will realize that many of the "mysteries of literature" may never become clear. If they did, they would cease to be mysteries. It is, I think, mysteries finely expressed for which we turn to literature. What may become clear to you in time is the beauty of mystery.

Then, just several days later, I received a typed note from a friend of Colleen's:

I talked to Colleen yesterday and she told me about her letter to you and your letter to her. It made me want to write to you, too, and tell you what I've been thinking. I have been getting increasingly frustrated with this class by the day. There are things I have loved about this class and things that have annoyed me. But I cannot point my finger on what I have learned or how, at the end of the year, I will sum up the entire year in one grade. I want to tell you the things that have frustrated me, not to criticize you, but so you can keep them in mind for next year's class.

At the beginning of the year you presented us with a brand new outlook on what English class could be like. I had my doubts, but after I heard how much time and thought you put into it, my hopes went up.

I remember that you wrote once about how you realized that a student of yours had wanted to learn, but on his own terms. Well, even if they were more traditional, I had my own ideas on how the class should run and I felt ignored and neglected.

Our class seemed to constantly adhere inflexibly to flexibility. We couldn't do anything without everyone's opinion, no matter how small and insignificant. So what could have been accomplished in one day was stretched over three or four days. But you never seemed to realize that you were the teacher and had license to break even the broken rules.

But I also want to take this time to thank you. Despite all my criticisms and struggles with this class, I've learned a lot about myself. My weakness with deadlines really came out this year; I had hoped to just ignore it as a problem. I know now I have to face it. I was able to pinpoint my own strengths and weaknesses in my writing, too.

I also understand how hard it is for a teacher to try to teach in a completely new way which students are not used to. You are a very patient and understanding man, and I believe that you will get very far with your students in the end.

Good luck.

I felt that it was important, as I wandered and experimented, to keep my colleagues and administrators informed of what I was doing and why I was doing it. I was concerned about how my work in the classroom might be interpreted by others if they did not understand what I was trying to do or that I was open to suggestion. Here is a letter I wrote to the superintendent, my department chair, and the director of curriculum and instruction:

These have been difficult days. My low-level students are unruly and my AP students are becoming anxious and impatient. One teacher told me I was arrogant to give students choice. Another told me that students need structure, much more than I am giving them. I keep thinking about that, and judging by the results, they may be right. And yet, I also wonder if one of the reasons the kids need so much structure is because it has always been created for them. I keep thinking I should be working at guiding them toward the creation of their own structures. I don't know.

One student boasted, today, of his ability to write A papers on books he never read. "I've been doing it for years!" That's a trick. But just a trick. What's harder, I think, is creating his own demands, challenging himself and meeting those challenges. I wonder what part I can play in teaching him how to do that.

I am writing now because I need a chance to catch my balance, if not my breath. I find myself leaving school shaken. I can't get my classes off my mind. What if I'm wrong? Surprisingly, though, even at my lowest moments, I continue to believe in what I am trying to do, though I keep questioning the way I go about it. I keep feeling an overwhelming desire to present my rationale to my students over and over again, to justify it, I suppose. But that's no good. That's meeting my needs, not theirs. I have to find ways to disconnect myself from their anxiety. I am now absorbing it.

I do sympathize with my students. I think of all the growing pains my own children have gone through in the past. My girls now want to go to movies alone and, at the same time, they want Mary and me to go with them. So we sit several rows behind them. "Leave me alone; stay with me." Like them and like my students, I continue to have that ambivalent feeling every time I reach for something new. "Let me try it my way; tell me what to do."

If I truly believe in what I am trying to do, I have to convey that confidence to my students and blend it with a genuine attentiveness to their concerns.

Reading these letters and others that I didn't include in this collection brings back the difficult days when I was not at all sure of what I was doing or going to do next; afraid, at times, that I had wandered too far from the path to places where nothing was recognizable. I remember that in my weakest moments, those times when my students probably needed me most, I wanted to return to my old ways—toughen up the discipline, have the kids meet me on my ground rather than work so hard to meet them on theirs, go back to the highly structured, monolithic essays, give grades, and trash the portfolios. In short, I wanted a vacation from thinking, to put my teaching on auto-pilot.

But I knew that I couldn't, in despair or frustration, toss it all out because it did not work for all, or because I hadn't yet figured out how to do it well. Criticism, even from one student, can seem loud, crushing. Sometimes, when I stepped back, I realized that the ones who were complaining were few in number. How could I have overlooked the smiling faces of the others? Indeed, I also received letters with comments like these:

> English has always been my hardest subject to grasp. But this year, you gave us a totally different perspective on life and writing; I believe this rubbed off on me and my writing style—for the better. We were not asked to write crap or just to write for the sake of writing; we were asked to write our feelings, our emotions, our thoughts. Never before had I been asked to do what I wanted, what I enjoyed, what I was good at. I was

encouraged to write quality pieces which meant something to me, not something for the teacher. And for the first time I was encouraged to take risks in my writing. No longer do I write to obtain an excellent grade, I write to enjoy the beauty and art of writing.

Ari Studnitzer

Before I took your class, I wrote to please the teacher. The five-paragraph essay was my forte, and I never had any problem getting A's in English. Then came the first day of school senior year and I was scared shitless after your class. How am I ever going to self-motivate myself to write four "completed" essays? Oh my God, why couldn't I have a regular teacher, I thought. First quarter was hard.

But then, slowly but surely, I became more sure of myself and my abilities. I began to treasure the enormous leeway you allowed us, and some works emerged which I will be proud to show my children. Ideas from my head caused teachers to cry and schoolmates to think and understand. I think these broken concepts were there all along, but it was you who taught me to put them together in a way that worked.

I have grown during this class as through no other. I feel blessed that I didn't have a regular teacher, bogged down with schedules and the conventional way. I took to heart the saying over your desk: *Make it true, make it clear.* You really affected me, Mr. Larson. I will never forget this class or the magnificent teacher who had the guts to teach it.

Janine N. Hill

So I worked at keeping my goals in mind: helping students to take responsibility for their education—getting them to think about what they were doing and how they were doing it, and to ask provocative, probing questions of themselves and of me. I wanted to find ways for them to make the important decisions, rather than doing it for them. But I had to find a way to do that without surrendering huge blocks of class time to unproductive conversation.

I learned that I have to listen with a clear head. Some students will fight me, and the reason may be because I changed all the rules on them. They feel vulnerable, uncertain whether they can perform as well as they always had. The challenge I present them with is an important one, I believe, but I have to be sensitive to their insecurity. Other students will complain for good reason. I probably did let discussions go astray too often and talked too much about what we were going to do. I offered too little guidance when they needed it. I am sympathetic to one student's well-worded concern that I "adhered inflexibly to flexibility."

But how to strike a balance? Maybe it has to do with being clear about my purpose. I think I have to be more interested in learning and growing than in being right. Maybe it's that simple. If I see everything that comes my way, even these letters that still hurt me to read, as contributing to my growth as a teacher, I will feel less threatened and remain more open to possibility. It is all, as Susan often told me, information.

So I turn the page now, relieved to move on, but glad to have revisited those disquieting days. I suppose that I should no sooner turn my back on my shortcomings than I should turn my back on the students who made me face them.

## Books I Wish I'd Known About at the Time

*Change Forces*, Michael Fullan
*What Do I Do Monday?* John Holt
*Embracing Contraries*, Peter Elbow
*There Are No Children Here*, Alex Kotlowitz
*Chasing Hellhounds*, Marvin Hoffman

# Conversations with Colleagues
## New Habits of Work

*For the kinds of change necessary to transform American education, the work force of teachers must do three tough things more or less at once: change how they view learning itself, develop new habits of mind to go with their new cognitive understanding, and simultaneously develop new habits of work—habits that are collegial and public in nature, not solo and private as has been the custom in teaching.*

Deborah Meier

My year began with the new superintendent's memo to me:

I was extremely pleased to hear about your work with portfolio assessment last spring. The reflective process you used was impressive. It demonstrated a true sensitivity to student learning. You may well have discovered a process worth repeating.

I certainly urge you to share your ideas and techniques with colleagues. Perhaps a small group of teachers could work together to experiment with various strategies. Please keep me posted on your efforts.

"I certainly urge you to share your ideas and techniques with your colleagues." The first time I read those words, I shuddered. Me? The very idea! Then shortly after I received Allan's memo, my department chair, Gene Stern, asked me to make a presentation of

my work with portfolios at the next department meeting. I turned
him down. Who was I to offer advice to these teachers? Some of
them had twenty-five to thirty years of experience. Some had been
teaching in this building when I was a student here, barely pulling
D's in most of my classes. Surely, there were others with ideas far
more significant, well formed, and time-tested than mine.

Our departmental gatherings had always been mercifully brief.
Gene ran through the list of agenda items as quickly as possible,
then we shared coffee and cookies or went our separate ways. We
liked it that way. All-school faculty meetings usually focused on
matters seemingly of little concern to anyone. Teachers, seated as
close to the back of the auditorium as possible, used the time to
grade papers, leaf through magazines, or sleep. This was the professional culture in which I was "growing up" as a teacher. The
"elders" were teaching me by their example that we teachers don't
often talk or think probingly about what we do. It's all I knew for the
first five years of my career, and it never occurred to me to challenge
that culture.

Then, after my experience in Susan's masters class—my first
experience where teachers shared thoughts and deep concerns,
asked hard questions, and together searched for answers—I hun-
gered for that level of engagement with my own colleagues. I was
beginning to realize that I didn't want to work in an environment
where people were disinclined to talk as professionals. To have an
idea and not share it, I now believed, perpetuated that culture.

So when Gene later asked me a second time, I did address the
department, along with two other teachers who had also been experimenting with portfolio assessment and nongraded work. And
though I was terrified, the session went well. Teachers asked
thoughtful questions and seemed interested.

In time, I would find myself addressing small groups of teachers,
district meetings, and university classes. But I never wanted to feel
singled out as a "presenter." I saw myself as one of many teachers
who were thinking and talking about teaching and learning. I put it
this way at the start of one staff development seminar:

> Sometimes people seem to want specific instructions, a game
> plan, a how-to manual, a recipe. I have found it is not easy to
> accommodate them. It has frustrated me, and I know it has frus-
> trated them. I think the reason I have not been able to accom-

modate these requests is because I should not. Each of my five classes and each student in each class is different and needs to be addressed in a different way. It is true of your classes too. I can no sooner recommend what you ought to do in the privacy of your classroom than I can or should recommend what you ought to wear. It must suit you. I think the emphasis should always be less on specifics than on, as Ted Sizer puts it, "the way we view adolescents, how they learn, and how we can help them deeply" (1992, 169). If we seriously examine and question the way we view our teaching, more effective ways of doing it will emerge.

Peter Elbow introduces his collection of essays, provocatively entitled *Embracing Contraries*, by saying he will not offer "things to do." Instead, he hopes his essays "can serve teachers by [. . .] setting up ways of looking at the learning and teaching process that will trigger in them specific things to do which they wouldn't otherwise have thought of" (1986).

When Gene retired after fifteen years as our chair, Carol Lounsbury, who was one of the teachers who presented portfolio assessment with me, took his place. She seemed determined from the start to get the English Department talking. She called a special session over the summer at which we brainstormed about what we wanted our classes to be like. During the year, in department meetings, she continued to open dialogue on some of our most difficult questions: Is our current curriculum useful and appropriate? Do we need our grammar tests? Can we explore alternative forms of assessment? How can we address the matter of low academic achievement of minority students? Because these issues are complex and controversial, and because solutions, at least for the moment, elude us, the conversations often made us uneasy and we sometimes became contentious. After one such meeting, I wrote this letter to the department:

> I was very pleased that we had the opportunity to talk. The importance of dialogue in our work can't be overstated, I think. In *The Power of Their Ideas*, Deborah Meier calls this "continuing dialogue face to face, over and over. . .a powerful educative force. . .our primary form of staff development" (1995, 109). I like to say that we are all each other's teachers.

I look forward to growing comfortable with and skilled at this conversation because it should never end, it should be our way of doing business. I am hopeful that these talks will not become battles between "my way" and "your way," the past and the present, or alternative assessments and grades. We are not looking for the "Right Way" so much as we are looking for what will be the most appropriate and constructive response to the needs of *these* students at *this* moment. We are groping toward what will work, what has meaning, what we value, why we value it, what we expect, why we expect it, and how we will measure whether students meet those expectations. Extremely important questions tend to go unanswered year after year. Until we learn to enter into the conversation fully and generously, most of our efforts will fall flat because they will not be founded on firm and common understandings.

We need to learn to do this together.

"Part II: Conversations with Colleagues" is a collection of letters that passed between my colleagues and me. Most of these letters, though they are addressed to individuals, were duplicated and shared with the rest of the department and the administration.

# Chapter Four

# Writing

*What we really want is to help youngsters learn how to express ideas of universal value in a personal voice.*
James Moffett

Now my students were writing more and were excited about what they were writing; their work was meaty, it was relevant, it was vivid, and it wasn't very good. Here is a typical example of the writing I was seeing:

### The Time I Was Almost the Victim of a Gang-related Shooting

It was a cool dark night in the middle of June when John and a few of his boys were on their way to the arcade and they had a large amount of money to play video games and to eat and shop at the mall. Before you think it, there's nothing wrong with John, he just had become a member of the Bloods, and the Bloods were the gang that was weak, desperate, and hated. Being a member of the Bloods is like committing suicide because even if you weren't killed by the other gang you would get hurt if you want to get out of the gang. When being a member of the Bloods getting jumped was the regular thing so that drove all of the Bloods to routinely carrying a gun. Their friend's name was TJ and TJ was a little crazy, he was the type of guy who would rob old ladies and sell drugs to pregnant women, when they would ask him why he did it he would just say, "It's just for the money."

John's friends that were with him were already starting to

converse with TJ asking him where he had been and where he was going and before John could say anything his friend Ben had invited TJ to go to the mall with them. TJ almost immediately said, "Hold on. Let me go get my strap!"

"Man, you don't need that gun," said John.

"Yo, man, cool out. There's something wrong, man, why is that car just sitting there in the middle of the street?"

"That's some fool creepin', TJ, we better get going," so John and his friends started to run as hard as they could down an alley when they noticed TJ hadn't run so they were all silent and they could hear TJ screaming gang-related slogans towards the car then suddenly they heard the cars music come on loud then the screech of the cars wheels on the pavement then what sounded like a large machine gun repeating fire into a mattress and the faint sound of a boy screaming suddenly then they heard the car stop with someone still shooting then the screech of the wheels again and then the gun went silent but the low rumble of a Marvin Gaye on the car stereo. John looked at his friends and they looked back at John they all had tears in their eyes and so did he, because they already knew what happened. They went back to see the mutilated body of their friend, the gangster TJ. This story is from my own experience and the only reason why I typed it up was to show what can happen at the spur of the moment with gangs.

Carl, the student who wrote this essay, couldn't wait for me to read it. "Man, check this out." He was excited because, as he said, "It sounds so real." I took that to mean that (1) he felt he had captured the reality of an incident, and/or (2) that it sounded like a "real" or professionally written essay. He had, of course, accomplished neither. I was glad that he was happy with his writing, but concerned that he was satisfied with it. I realized then that I was not communicating a standard clearly.

I got many essays like Carl's: raw, unfocused, confusing, badly punctuated, riddled with poor grammar and spelling, but real and, often, honest and intense. What to say to Carl? How to teach form, structure, mechanics without violating the piece he had in mind?

I face this dilemma often. Recently, Tanya, an African-American senior, was working on an essay about something terrible her mother had done that Tanya believed she had to own up to and admit to her sister. Tanya's standard English needed work, so we sat side by side, going through the piece. I read sentences to her like, "She got no more sense then a dog" and she smiled to hear that construction from my lips. Because the essay was supposed to be a formal piece, she changed it. But, then we came to the climactic moment in the piece where she was insisting that her mother tell her sister what had happened. "'Cause if she don't I will," Tanya had written. I read it aloud, and Tanya didn't smile. I asked, "How does that sound to you?"

"Good," she said, then smiled.

I told her that the rest of the piece was more formal so we probably shouldn't use "cause." I read her my version: "Because if she doesn't, I will." Tanya frowned.

I said, "You want to leave it, don't you?"

"Kinda, yeah," she said.

"Why?"

"Because I want it to sound strong," she said.

I had to admit that her way did sound stronger, more emphatic. I was stuck. Again.

Like Tom Romano, I had read "many samples of writing from government officials, lawyers, and school and hospital administrators that were wordy, pompous, vague, mealy-mouthed, and perfectly edited" (1987, 75). On the other hand, I had also read many strong student essays whose impact was sorely damaged by errors large and small. I knew that getting my kids excited about what they wrote wasn't my whole job. But uncertain of how to proceed as I read their papers, I found myself waffling between editing and nurturing, unable to blend the two. I offered encouragement for what students had done well, sometimes gushing about the "importance" of the work; then I dipped my pen in red ink and went to work "correcting" the piece. I couldn't seem to stop myself.

## How Do I Proceed?

Carl's essay presents an interesting and, for me, common problem: As he retells what happened after John and "his boys" see the car, he stops punctuating entirely. This creates some confusion for the reader, but if it were done well, the device could make for an interesting passage. One image runs into the next, just as such an event might be remembered. I can see the film running in his head while he wrote.

To be honest, however, I suspect that this passage is more likely a result of carelessness and lack of skill than an attempt at style; and yet, it's also possible that, regardless of whether Carl realizes it consciously or not, that passage may be part of what made him want me to "check it out quick." With those possibilities in mind, I wonder— Do I help him punctuate that section "correctly" or do I try to find a way to get him to articulate the effect he had in mind, even if he had discovered it accidentally, then help him find ways to achieve it without losing his reader? Do I write in correct punctuation and hope he understands why I made the changes? Do I try to arrange a writing conference? Do I give a failing grade and tell him to rewrite? Do I give him a split grade, say, one for impact and one for mechanics? I'd tried it all.

Then a young English teacher named Fred Schenck handed me an article, by Richard Straub, on teacher response to writing that appeared in CCC May (1996, 223). I wrote to Fred and distributed that letter to other colleagues:

> I want to thank you for showing me Straub's article. It came at a good time. I've grown dissatisfied with the way I mark my kids' writing. I vacillate between not doing enough and doing way too much in the way of circling errors, crossing out words and replacing them with choices of my own, and making comments like, "move this here," and "omit this paragraph." Sometimes I don't even bother to explain why.
>
> I worry that I'm acting more as their editor or proofreader than as their writing teacher. When my own editor orders that I *condense* or *delete*, I know it is because he wants to help me (us) get a finished product as soon as possible. When he circles typos or crosses out words and replaces them with others, I simply call up the chapter on my computer and make the changes. It takes two minutes. It's not very instructive, but it's not meant to be. That seems a different objective from the one I ought to have in mind as I read kids' work.
>
> I probably make highly directive comments on their papers for a selfish reason. I want that draft to be "completed" and ready for the portfolio quickly. My haste may rob my kids of chances to, as Straub puts it, "get more practice in [their] writ-

ing processes and more comfortable making decisions as a writer." In other words, I make their revision decisions for them. I find I have the most fun and learn more as a writer when an editor's comments nudge me toward something different, but not something in particular.

I agree with Newkirk [cited in Straub's article] who wants to strike a balance between two opposing mandates: "(1) to evaluate and suggest revision, and (2) to encourage the student to take initiative, to take control of the paper" (249). Yeah, but how?

I'd like to start by heeding Straub's final bit of advice and "take a close, hard look at the comments we make, consider whether they are doing what we want them to do, and make whatever changes we can to make them better" (248). We should try to get together a group of teachers, preferably with different approaches to evaluating writing and ideally from a variety of departments, who would be interested in meeting periodically to practice "grading" papers.

Another colleague of mine, Anny Heydeman, who had taught at Evanston for twenty-four years, chided me from time to time for not paying enough attention to matters of form. She had seniors who had been in my junior class whom she felt I had not prepared sufficiently. A letter she had written to me earlier about a former student of mine echoed in my head as I read Carl's essay.

I have told several people about two specific students who are in my classes this year. Neither of them began the year writing idiomatic English, since both of them learned English as a second language. Therefore, they wrote incorrectly, mainly in the use of verb forms. They both came into my class believing that no other English teacher cared about these mistakes. I can't believe that these students had never received any help, but if they did, it did not register.

This is not a minor issue. There are many more negative consequences in the real world for people who do not write correctly than there are for people who do not write from their soul. That statement sounds more "snippy" than I feel, but I do believe the content. The most basic application becomes flawed when it is misspelled, written in careless handwriting, and written with bad mistakes in usage and grammar. I don't want the demands of the workplace to dictate our whole curriculum, but I think we cheat our students if we send them into the world thinking that mistakes in form are trivial.

Whatever we decide to do about correct grammar and spelling should be the result of a conscious, department-wide policy, so students do not feel confused about different standards, or expectations.

I agree with Anny. Mechanical correctness is not a small matter. But I also had seen many kids needlessly intimidated by persnickety teachers to the point of never wanting to write for fear of making an error. Case in point: I once told one of our administrators that it might be interesting to see him write down and distribute his thoughts to the staff from time to time as a way of encouraging teachers to be more reflective. He balked at the idea because "all I can think about is how time-intensive it would be." I assured him it didn't have to take more than an hour every few weeks to put his thoughts on paper; surely, the work didn't have to be perfect. But he confessed concern about the idea of twenty-nine pairs of English teachers' eyes reading his work. I think that's a shame. I believe school may have taught him to be afraid. The result, in this case, was not clarity or attention to detail as we sometimes like to think, but reluctance to write at all.

But the question remains: How to move Carl to the next step? Or better yet, what *is* the next step? Clearly, he wanted to tell this story and he liked what he had written. Just as clearly, the piece suffered from a lack of focus and mechanical correctness. How could I take Carl's interest and energy and help him write a better piece? What should I, as his teacher, tinker with and what should I leave alone? I was interested in both the nature and timing of my interventions.

## Toward Personal Voice and Precision

While reading Mike Rose's *Possible Lives*, I became fascinated by the comments of Steve Gilbert, one of the teachers Rose profiles in the book. Steve says, in part, "As a teacher, I want people to have their voice respected, and I want to help people arrive at a sense of their value and worth" (181). That caught my eye. Later, Steve tells Rose about teaching *As I Lay Dying* and how some of the students disliked one of the characters, Dewey Dell. Gilbert says that, as far as he's concerned, it's all right for students never to like Dewey Dell, but adds that if they "can *listen* to Dewey Dell and judge her from a position of understanding, from inside her language. . .well, that's something" (187). I broadened the idea for my own purposes to include students understanding themselves and each other in the same way, "from a position inside their language," and grew excited by the possibilities of that stance, as opposed to my usual stance as their language doctor.

I wrote to Steve Gilbert about my interest in balancing respect for student voice with getting kids to write with clarity and a sense of audience and purpose. He replied, saying he agreed that these two aspirations need not be mutually exclusive:

> I would like to speak briefly on your consideration about "what it would do for kids' understanding of themselves and who they are in this world, if they could get inside their own language." It is an idea which interests me also. For me, it is one of the ethical principles of the job, and I "attack" it directly. I want kids to hear what they are actually saying and also to retain control over their speech. One of the reasons that I try to get students to be precise as they state ideas is that it makes it easier for them to retain control of their own ideas. Too often at imprecise moments, when a teacher reframes a student's idea, I find the original language ideas are lost. Related to this, I also think that in our desire to create "perfect essays," we, as teachers, too often erase voice. Students are then discouraged from allowing their own voices to enter their papers. Again, I find that only when voice is in a paper, is the paper any good.
>
> I don't think this desire for students to write in their own voice in any way contradicts a desire for precision in speaking or writing. With my students I have a number of assignments (which somehow produce papers with lots of voice), and through them, I try to blur the distinction between creative and expository writing. When the borders get sufficiently blurred, I get better papers. I guess these ideas grow from a respect for voice and a feeling that marginalized voices are too often effaced. Try to work directly with encouraging students to respect their own language.

## Discovering a Clue to the Next Step

I received a paper written by a junior student, Lambert "Cool" Sayles, Jr., in which he described his uncle's mistreatment at the hands of the police. The essay, "CRooKeD CoPs," was vivid, hilarious in places, and absolutely true to life. Lambert even managed to work himself and his own interviewing methods into the piece, which doesn't seem a wholly unreasonable thing to do, given the way television reporters today find ways to spotlight themselves in the telling of someone else's story.

On Saturday, May 4, 1996, I sat down with my uncle at home and asked him a couple questions about his run-ins with the cops in his younger days. He was in a rush, so I had to make it quick. I told him just to tell me a little something about cops and how they're crooked, and he said

"Well I'm going to tell you about the time me and Bibzee. . ."

". . .Our cousin Bibzee," I said.

"Yeah, fool, who else would I be talking about named Bibzee?" he said.

"Man dude I'm trying to interview you man, the person that might read this don't know no Bibzee."

I must say I loved reading Lambert's essay. I read it over several times, enjoying its rhythm and true-to-life dialogue. His voice throughout the piece was authentic and, I felt, well suited to the material he meant to convey.

Lambert loves to write, but I know that he needs help writing in standard English. And yet, I also know that writing this essay in standard English would, to use Steve Gilbert's word, "erase" Lambert's voice and probably diminish the impact of the piece. Then I discovered a clue to the next step within Lambert's essay.

I'd been stressing in class the important link between audience and purpose. I showed my students many examples of published and student writing, and we talked about what the author's purpose might have been. Then we talked about whether the author had achieved his purpose and how he had or why he hadn't.

I noticed that Lambert had a sense of audience in his essay ("Man dude. . .the person that might read this don't know no Bibzee."). I asked Lambert how he wanted this essay to sound and he said, "Like me." And that it did. When I read it, I could hear

Lambert's voice as clearly as if he were reading it to me. But what about the matter of clarity? Long stretches of the essay were difficult to understand because they were so badly punctuated and written in Black English Vernacular. So I asked Lambert, "What if you wanted the police to read this to know how your uncle felt? Or what if you wanted to draw public attention to the problems African-American males sometimes encounter when they are stopped by the police? Would that change your writing?" He quickly replied that it would. He said he'd want it to sound more "proper" (his word). And this gave me an opportunity to show him how he might do that. He wrote two versions of this essay for his file, each appropriate in its own context.

## Relevance Is Important But Is It Enough?

I've found that important topics and real audiences make an enormous difference in students' writing. I work hard to find real reasons for students to write: letters to editorial pages or to politicians, speeches and presentations for other classes, etc. The piece has to matter to the student. After the LA riots, for example, our class discussions and the subsequent essays grew more angry every day. It wasn't long before they became repetitive; anger chased anger. So I had the kids write a letter to Dr. Martin Luther King, Jr. Though they had no trouble considering the late Dr. King an audience, I knew I couldn't let these letters just sit in their files. They had to go somewhere and be read. So I told the kids I'd send them to the Martin Luther King National Center for Non-Violent Social Change in Atlanta. I'd already talked to a woman there who said she'd pass the letters on to King's sister.

The resulting writings surprised me. Few of my students wrote about the riots. They let go of the anger and reached, in their writing, the underlying pain, the feelings of betrayal, confusion, helplessness that may have been the source of much of the outrage. Interestingly, few students even mentioned the riots specifically; many, instead, focused on matters closer to home. Three kids in our community had been murdered over the course of two years, and that was on their minds, moreso than I had realized.

Here is a sampling of excerpts from their letters. They all began, "Dear Dr. King":

What is the world coming to? Why did you have to go? If you were still here you could make one of your famous speeches about how everybody should overcome and be as one. I really don't know what is happening. From the last two years in Evanston and in the world, I've witness thousands of people getting shot or killed or hurt and I just keep wondering if I am next!

I'm just a freshman. If there was some way for me to stop all this problems, I would do so. My mom told me that when she was little she could walk the streets at night without worry in her mind. I can't walk the streets at daytime without fear.

Two more kids was killed in Evanston. I can't believe my eyes.

I think we are getting too violent. Some kids are so eager to fight that they will ride up beside you on a bike and kick at you, ram you, cut you off, and steal things from you, even if you are on a tricycle.

We as a country are failing. In Evanston the funeral and burial service of a teenager killed wasn't quite over before a second killing happened. The first was a shock, but to have two of us die in a month almost killed us. There is no reason for Mike, Marchelle, and now Tommy to be six feet under. More killings of more teenagers means no next generation.

You had a dream that the people of the world would unite. For a moment I thought your dream was going to come true.

Relevance is extremely important. It is a means to getting at what the kids have an urgency to write. When they write with urgency, the writing, very often, is better. But is relevancy enough? Grant Wiggins says that we often fail to hear students' request for "more *meaning* in their work (as opposed to relevance). There are many instructional and assessment challenges that are not relevant to students' immediate practical concerns and interests" (1993, 44).

My colleagues frequently (and rightfully) remind me that our kids need to be prepared to write for the workplace, to draw up clear proposals and write precise business letters. And many kids need to be prepared for college writing. I once wrote to Fred and confessed that "it gives me a pang to see your commitment to teaching kids to write for college and the workplace. I probably don't do that nearly enough. Anny's voice is always in my head, as it should be. She too has an eye on where many of the kids are headed: college and analytic writing. I don't discount the importance of that type of writing. I'm just always wondering how to make it viable, interesting, real, necessary to the kids. I must work harder on that."

Anny wrote:

> We need to spend some serious time and effort discussing the role of analytic thinking and writing. In my set of assumptions, that kind of thinking is not only the basis of all scholarship in all disciplines, but also a technique that I hope they will apply as they form judgments in all areas of their lives. We need to understand when we are operating on a huge, comforting generalization, such as "democracy is better than communism," that the sentence doesn't mean anything without specific definitions of both terms. In my experience, teenagers often seem to avoid breaking down their fondly held assumptions. I'm the same way. Why would I want to learn any facts that might disturb my prejudices? Fighting to make a dent in this armor of dependence on conventionally accepted wisdom seems to me one of the most important jobs of all educational institutions.
>
> But unfortunately, being analytical seems to have become tainted and the opposite of being creative and working toward the most powerful expression possible. That position worries me a great deal. One of my continual goals is to alert students to the fact that thinking and feeling are not mutually exclusive. The degree to which the students' work is only generated by their desires is a problem for me. I believe that we are being self-indulgent if we only want students to enjoy and appreciate language and never help them use the language in other contexts.

I responded somewhat defensively, probably because I was beginning to see my position deteriorating:

> Like you, Anny, I want my students to think and write ana-
> lytically—all the time. I try to get my kids to talk about their
> lives, our world, how the two engage, and what they are read-
> ing and writing. Through modeling and discussion, I strive to
> get them to support their opinions with specifics, over and over
> again. And to think about what they're thinking. But I may do
> this in a less formal way than I used to. Instead of saying, as I
> used to, "Where's your support?" or "Where are our three exam-
> ples?" I now simply ask, "Why do you think that? Help me
> understand your thinking." It's the same end as you have in
> mind, I believe.

I like what Grant Wiggins has to say in this regard: "The teacher who is interested enough to ferret out what we are thinking, who persists in trying to understand our unexpected and opaque answers [. . .] ultimately provides powerful incentive for us to develop the self-discipline required to refine our thinking and our answers" (108).

## Bringing It All Together

So I had all of these seemingly conflicting objectives in mind—I wanted to respect and nurture students' voices and I wanted to "ele-vate," where needed, their speaking and writing; I hoped to create assignments of high interest to them but also give them plenty of experiences with the sort of writing required in college and the working world. I searched for an idea that would meld these ideas in a single project.

Then one day, I heard a program on National Public Radio's "All Things Considered." The program was "Remorse: The Thirteen Stories of Eric Morse." It had been created by two teenagers, LeAlan Jones and Lloyd Newman, who live a block away from the Ida B. Wells housing project where five-year-old Eric Morse was dropped to his death from a twelfth-story window. His two assailants were, at the time of the murder, eleven and twelve years old. LeAlan and Lloyd contacted producer David Isay, for whom they had created a radio program in 1993 called "Ghetto Life 101." They told Isay they wanted to "tell the story behind the story" of Eric's death. For a year they worked on this project, interviewing residents of Ida B. Wells, relatives of the killers, and Vince Lane, then-chairman of the Chicago Housing Authority; they even spoke to Eric's mother in the only interview she granted to the press.

People Magazine ran a story on the two young men and mentioned the names of their schools. I contacted LeAlan through his school and arranged for him to meet with my classes. He spent an entire day with us; what was supposed to be an intimate talk turned into a large assembly as more and more teachers wanted to bring their classes to hear him speak.

In conjunction with his visit, I created an assignment called Stories That Must be Told and asked students to "go out into their world and find a story that you feel needs to be told." (See Appendix C for the parameters of the assignment.) Students were expected to discover a true story for which they could attain first-hand information and to tell it twice: The first telling had to be an objective and carefully researched narrative of the events; the second telling was supposed to be subjective—students were free to tell it in any way that interested them and to show off their unique talents. In the end, for the second telling, I received videos, radio shows, paintings, a series of photos, short stories, songs, and a dramatic monologue.

When we first started the project, it took me a while to convince students that (1) there were many stories available to them in their world, and (2) that I didn't want a paper that they had to go to the library to write. I wanted a story that forced them to interact with the world, to take a real incident and recreate it with words. Students worked toward a precise, objective first telling, then explored the same material in any way that seemed most appropriate to them. This was a way for me to show that I value both forms of expression.

I believe it is probably a sad reflection on our times that six of my students wrote about the violent deaths of relatives or friends. Other stories ranged in subject matter from a girl's encounters with a series of foster homes to a successful fifty-year marriage. I found that once students were engaged in what they were doing and once that distinction between expository and creative writing was, as Steve Gilbert said, blurred, their investment in the quality of the project increased dramatically.

The project had the added benefit of creating some very real audiences. Two girls, for example, interviewed parents and teachers about what Evanston was like when the schools first became integrated in the sixties. For their second telling, they probed on videotape the question, "Is Evanston really integrated today?" They found and filmed shocking disparities between the racial makeup of advanced and remedial classes. The administration became aware of the film, viewed it, and considered showing it to the board. One of the girls, Carrie Abrams, became so interested in what she found that she went on to write a speech about the unfairness of tracking and, after gathering all her courage, presented it during "pubic forum" at a school-board meeting.

Another student, Beverly, wrote about the murder of her brother. When she first mentioned the idea in class, I could see that the topic made her emotional. I asked her several times whether she really wanted to do that story. I wondered how she would be able to tell it objectively. She insisted that she did want very much to tell it. Eventually, her entire family became involved in the telling of this story; relatives called her, she said, and wanted to be interviewed. She even attended the trial of the man accused of the murder and incorporated her observations in the paper. Beverly visited Fred's freshman classes (which were also working on the same project) and talked to them about how she had approached the work. By the second time she addressed one of these classes, she was offering the freshmen advice! When the paper was finished, her mother hung it proudly on her bedroom door.

## Getting Closer to the Point

So I had, at least for the moment, found a way to bring together voice and precision, to let kids choose their own work but within certain parameters, to engage them in their work while they learned techniques of active research, and to see their world as a place rich with stories.

As I worked on constructing this project, talking frequently with Fred and another teacher, Warren Wolfe, who did it with their classes, I was fascinated to find myself beginning to tighten the parameters of the assignment more and more. Not long ago I would have fought against that urge, thinking it was a nasty remnant of my old teaching impulses. In this situation, I felt comfortable saying, "I am your producer. Both of our names go on this project so I won't let you slide with mediocre work." And "video and radio presentations must be twelve minutes long—no longer, no shorter." After all, that's about how long most television news-magazine stories last. Professionals work within parameters. I was wrong to give kids as much leeway as I had given them in the past. Or, more precisely, I was wrong to give them so much latitude in every area of the work. Perhaps if I let them find their topics and their own means of conveying their material, I could and should establish a framework within which this "freedom" is exercised. Paulo Freire, in *We Make the Road by Walking*, says that "the teacher has to teach, to *demonstrate* authority, and the student has to experience freedom in relation to the teacher's authority (1990, 61)." I was beginning to see that my "authority" and their "freedom" did not have to be in conflict.

Nancie Atwell's book *In The Middle* had taught me a lot about the power of student choice, so when I met her I told her that I had taken much of what I learned from her book to the high school. Then I told her how curious I was to find myself going back to more specificity in my expectations. I liked her reply.

"It's not a matter of going back," Nancie said. "It's a matter of getting closer to the point."

## Books I Wish I'd Known About at the Time

*Will My Name Be Shouted Out?*, Steven Carter
*We Make the Road by Walking*, Myles Horton and Paulo Freire,
    ed. Brenda Bell, John Gaventa, and John Peters
*Democracy and Education*, John Dewey
*Education and Experience*, John Dewey
*What Is English?*, Peter Elbow
*Bird by Bird*, Anne Lamott

# Chapter Five

# Reading

*Those who cram the classics down students' throats long before they are ready are careless of the fate of the great works of the past. Even if the majority were to graduate from high school without having encountered many of the great authors, we should not need to be alarmed if they had the ability to read with understanding and had acquired a zest for the experience that literature can give.*

*Those who try to crowd into the school years everything they "ought" to read evidently assume that the youth will never read again after school years are over. People who read for themselves will come to the classics at the point when particular books have particular significance for them.*

Louise M. Rosenblatt

After figuring out our taxes last year, my wife Mary announced to me that we'd spent over twelve hundred dollars on books. We both love books and love to read. Our parents are readers and we hope our children will be readers too. As a teacher then, it pained me to see my students opening some of my favorite books as if they suspected the volumes were booby-trapped. Asking them to read was like asking them to perform some awful chore, like cleaning their room or mowing the lawn. "Aw, God no!", they cried. I wondered why.

Of course, I first lined up the usual suspects: television, laziness, computers, their previous teachers; then I rebuked the culprits in the usual ways: "If only you. . .then I could do magical things with my kids." But that never moved us forward. No matter how much blame I tossed around, my students continued to come to class unprepared and unconcerned. "I don't have time to read they said," or "This book is stupid" or "Why can't we read something good? Like Terry McMillan?"

At my worst, I'd just shrug my shoulders and let the kids fail. "Hey, I gave you fair warning." At my best, I'd intensify my usual methods: more quizzes, harder quizzes, more frequent tests, and sterner lectures about the dangers of not reading: "I'll call your parents" or "You'll fail." But what did any of this have to do with giving them a good reason to read or with instilling in them a desire to read or helping them create a habit of reading? Something in the way I brought reading to my classroom had to change.

## Starting Over

I started by asking myself what I hoped my students would get from or be able to do with their reading. Ideally, I reckoned, they would first find pleasure in the reading. I'd also like them to be able to make connections between their reading and their own experiences, with the hope that making those connections would enhance their understanding of their experiences. I'd like them to be able to view reading as a way of broadening their world, as well as an effective way to relax. And I'd like them to be able to read for information. That seemed like plenty of goals with which to start.

Once I looked at my wish list for students, I realized that the way I taught most books achieved none of those ends, at least not to a significant degree. I was horrified to realize how much time and energy I devoted to policing their reading, making sure that they didn't come unprepared or with *Cliff's Notes* stuffed in their hip pockets. But with what would I replace those reading quizzes, tests, and discussions of theme and conflict?

I looked again at my own reading habits. Some books, I realized, I read slowly. Annie Dillard's work, for example, I like to read slowly. With other books, like true crime (a particular sinful passion of mine), I skip parts, skim others, read and reread thoroughly still others. It all depends on what I want to get from a book. There are, obviously, many reasons and ways to read. But it occurred to me that I had been expecting one type of reading from my students: cover-to-cover, lock-step readings during which students prepared to answer *my* questions, some of which covered minute details. The conscientious students read for the purpose of passing the quiz or to have something to say when I called on them during discussions. They didn't read to have their eyes opened or to be carried away. Those students who didn't care about the quiz—and there were many—didn't read.

## Reading Through the Teacher's Eyes

At the start of one school year, I opened my classes with a conversation on what it is like to read for school. One student confessed to me that he always did his readings for classes but never enjoyed it because "I was reading through the teacher's eyes." Another student said that he too always kept up with reading, but never got to "see the book" because he was having to read so fast to keep up with the schedule. When I asked him how I could make this year's reading experience different, he shrugged and said he guessed he just wanted to be able to see the book.

I realized I wanted to create a room full of (if you'll pardon my jargon) life-long readers rather than, as before, readers of this particular book at this particular time in this particular manner. I wanted to get kids to pay attention to their own reading habits so that counterproductive habits could be modified, and so they could recognize what worked for them and build on that. I wanted them to read through their own eyes and to see the book. Most of all, I wanted them to read because they wanted to read.

First, I had to stop being the reading cop. That wasn't easy. The impulse was ingrained. Instead of check-up quizzes (Grant Wiggins calls them "Gotcha!" quizzes), I tried having my students respond briefly in writing to an open-ended question on what they had read: "Tell me what you think was the most important moment in this chapter and why you think it's important." Everyone in the room turned in a paper. If students were unable to respond to a question, they were obligated to explain why. There was no penalty so they could be honest. Yesterday's absentees told me why they were absent and when they planned to make up the question. Students who had fallen behind in their reading explained why and either told me what they planned to do differently or how they would avoid the problem in the future. Sometimes they asked me for advice. Those who read but were perplexed by what they had read, wrote about their confusion and asked me questions. I responded briefly to their inquiries and reacted to their comments. Thus, I had a written dialogue going with them about what they were reading. When we finished the book, they added a cover sheet to all of their responses where they reflected on how the reading of this book had gone for them. Finally, they stapled all the pages together: a reading journal.

Their reflections were very interesting to me. For example, Nickie wrote, "I started out liking *Hiroshima* a whole lot, but then it started getting technical, so I wasn't able to stay interested. I wasn't able to answer for two days in a row. But at Chapter Four I got interested again and ended up reading ahead of you all because it got better." When it came time for to me evaluate her work on the unit, I would have hated to have to average in the two F's Nickie would have gotten for those two days when she lost interest. I was more interested in her overall work on the book, her attitude toward it, engagement with it, and her attention to her own reading habits.

## In Search of Ways to Allow Students to Read Through Their Own Eyes

I'd returned to Nancie Atwell's *In the Middle* and wondered how a reading workshop would go over in a high school classroom. I'd seen for myself how students behaved better in an atmosphere that didn't assume they were up to no good. I'd seen how much better they performed when I gave them some leeway to read at their own pace. What if I let them choose their own books, and set their own reading pace, at least once? Of course, I worried about what I would do with class time, what I would do if the kids chose junk, and how my colleagues would respond. And, of course, the reading cop in me railed against the idea. But I thought it was worth a try and gave three weeks to letting kids read in class.

Some of the kids got so interested in their own chosen reading that they read at home, moved on to other books, recommended books to each other, sought recommendations from friends and family members, and eagerly urged me to read their books. For the first time, there was a real excitement about reading in my room, exactly what I'd been looking for. Yes, there were kids reading novels that I might consider lesser works: John Grisham, Anne Rice, and Terry McMillan. But there were also students who discovered, for example, the work of Samuel Beckett and Cornel West and Jane Austin. The following quarter, I gave them *Catcher in the Rye*. But their resistance to the idea of a common reading was stronger than ever. One student said, "You're just a teacher again!" So I toyed with the idea of turning the whole quarter over to independent reading and discussed the possibility with my classes.

One day on my way to lunch, a colleague stopped me and said, "I can't believe what I just heard. Somebody told me you trashed the curriculum." So I wrote this rationale and delivered it to the mailboxes of my English Department colleagues:

> I try what I try because I want to be a better teacher. I certainly don't want to do more harm than good. So I have concerns. One concern has been raised by some of you. It's about the canon, and whether I am losing sight of it. I worry about that too and would like to share my thoughts with you. I don't have answers. I'm searching. I need your wisdom.
>
> Harold Bloom (1994) and Nancie Atwell (1987) do battle in my brain every day. On the one hand I see, as does Bloom, that there must be a body of works to which our children are exposed. Literature is like cultural DNA, it carries built-in information about where we've been and how we ought to conduct our lives. It also gives us common frames of reference—not a bad thing in an increasingly fragmented world—as well as standards for quality work. And beyond that, it's just good stuff that enriches the soul.
>
> On the other hand, thanks to Atwell, I see that the way I had been teaching these works was too often damaging to students' desire to read. In my zeal to pass on a literary heritage that I valued, I sometimes lost sight of the interests and insights of individual students, that which makes Sally Sally and not Anne . . . and certainly not me. So I began wondering what would happen if I let the kids find their own way, guided and prompted now and then by me.
>
> If we do want a canon in which we can believe so thoroughly that we are compelled to pass it on to our children, shouldn't we be putting some extended time and energy into an examination of it? If it's specific and reasonably agreeable to all, our first and ongoing responsibility to the kids (and to the canon) might be to help our kids understand why this or that book is in the canon. We also ought to be having continuing conversations with them about why a canon is important in the first place. We should invite them to argue with our rationale and

question the canon and, eventually, with luck, they will begin to formulate for themselves what should stay and what should go and be able to articulate why. As it is, I have a feeling that what we consider a canon appears to the kids an unrelated series of overly precious works that are only read in school—possibly even, as one student suspected, written for the sole purpose of torturing school children, like grammar exercises.

Is it fair to ask students to assume *a priori* what we have already assumed for them: These are great books? When the kids appear not to agree (Gatsby is boring!), we are appalled or confused, sometimes even hurt (How can it be boring? It's Gatsby! There must be something wrong with *you*.).

The kids are definitely on to us. That's no secret. If there is a way to pass a quiz or test without reading, they'll find it. That becomes the intellectual challenge, and they do like intellectual challenges, I've found. But I'd rather challenge them to find a book with which they would love to spend time and to which they would eagerly return in the still moments of their lives. I'd love for them to read closely, freely reacting to it, both in writing and in conversation, or, for that matter, in any other way that makes sense to them. I want them to want others to read what they've read because it meant that much to them. Isn't that impulse at the heart of a literary canon?

What if we saw ourselves as keepers not of the flame of literary heritage, but of the flame of the desire to read? I really wonder if that might increase the chances that important works will continue to be read. I believe that the canon is far more resilient than our children's desire to read. If I had to choose to preserve one over the other, I'd certainly choose to preserve the latter.

Anny replied to my letter saying she wanted to "make a strong plea in favor of the continuation of requiring some titles every year and also the teaching of some books to the whole class as a group." She had tried a unit in which she gave students an opportunity to read a book of his or her own choosing. Each student was expected to read two hundred pages and write two papers, one creative and one an analytic paper about the book. "This was a very successful unit," she reported. "The reading became self-directed and the writing assignments worked very well. I saw several students demonstrate, some for the first time, a kind of analytic thinking that I believe is the heart of most scholarship: supporting a general idea by using specific references. It is exciting for both of us when the students make this cognitive leap." However, she added,

> . . . at the end of that unit, we worked on *Streetcar Named Desire* together, and that experience convinced me that students need class discussion about a shared reading experience as much as they need chances to read books that they have chosen themselves. During our discussion, we worked through some of the passages that the students had not "gotten" on their own. The students had not realized that Stanley was not hostile to Blanche when she first arrived, that Blanche lied selectively, or even that Stanley raped Blanche. They needed our group work to be able to begin to think about the play on their own.
>
> Helping students find what the author meant is only one, really quite basic, stage in the appreciation of literature. If students only read works they have chosen themselves, we miss the chance to lead students into literature they would not have chosen for themselves, but which they will be happy to have encountered.
>
> Students, especially those who already read for pleasure, enjoy challenges. I like doing this kind of teaching, and many students enjoy this kind of learning. For me, the art of teaching is to present students with a task that is harder than they thought they were capable of doing and to work with them so that they can accomplish this task. Learning that reading is often a pleasure is essential. But while I do want students to enjoy reading, I also want them to understand that the enjoyment of a work of literature is not the only end possible. My pleasure is not the highest standard of value, and to be taught that it is seems solipsistic to me.
>
> Perhaps you have gathered that I think the canon is worth saving. These books ask the deepest, most important questions: Do we have free will? What is the nature of humankind? Can society be changed? Through our collective reading of the classics, we can help students see alternatives to the assumptions they probably don't even know they have accepted. I believe we must continue to perform that function.

I responded to Anny:

> I was very pleased to receive your thoughtful letter. It has

changed my thinking somewhat. You have reminded me of the value of whole-group discussions of books. I do miss them. I'm trying to find a way to make them work, really work, for as many kids as possible, not just those select few who always tend to participate. And don't get me wrong, I haven't trashed the canon, I've just questioned it.

I disagree, however, that "helping students find out what the author had in mind is. . .a really basic stage in the appreciation of literature". I think of Samuel Beckett's response to an often-asked question: "If I knew who Godot was," he said, "I'd have said so in the play" (Bair 1978, 382).

Recently, my AP kids ran up against an interesting problem. They decided that if they had read *Waiting for Godot* in manuscript form on their own, they would have thought it was "crap." Because it was published and because I had given it to them in a class, they assumed it had some specific value. What that value was they could not articulate. I asked them what they would do if they were a first reader for a publishing house and theirs were the first eyes to see *Waiting for Godot* or *Catch 22* or *Grendel*. How would they determine the value of these books? Those twenty-six students went silent. They are better at trying to guess what the author had in mind than in articulating how the work struck their own minds.

But this incident also raises an interesting matter: When I allow kids to read works in class that some adults might consider objectionable or of low literary merit, I have *de facto* placed a stamp of approval on it. I need to be aware of that. Letting kids read whatever they want tells them, in a sense, that all writing is, in some way, equal. Drawing distinctions between works of quality and lesser works is important, even if we ultimately disagree. I think John Grisham is a bland writer; reasonable adults may disagree. But we ought, at least, to have the conversation; that opportunity, for the moment, is not available in my classroom.

Carol, our department chair, brought up the issue of the canon at a department meeting. Later, Fred and I talked about our concern that the department conversation was moving too swiftly toward creating a list of books before we had really talked about the function of such a list. We put out a joint memo that read, in part:

We believe that an important reason for having students read, and possibly having them read certain works in particular, is to maintain a cultural tradition. The question becomes, "Who determines the cultural tradition?" Any shared experiences that we, as a department, decide the faculty and students should have become illustrative examples of what we believe the school, our community, is. How do we approach the monumental task of defining ourselves?

Laura Cooper, our director of curriculum and instruction, responded to our memo and refined our questions:

I have mixed feelings about "another" canon debate. I am, however, interested in a question about knowledge and skills and habits of mind we think are essential for competent readers/thinkers. . .then, we can "plan backwards" to design curriculum and instruction.

## Turn to the Kids

Fred, who had done his student teaching under Anny, told me he sometimes finds himself torn between my point of view and Anny's. The truth is, I often look to him for guidance because his perspective seems to me to be not moderate, but more reasoned than either mine or Anny's. Anny is a Harvard grad; I was a college drop out. Anny is proud of what she has accomplished in the academic world and values what school has always had to offer. My own education left me skeptical and angry. We both bring our own presuppositions to our arguments. Fred is able to arrive at his own point of view without all the assumptions that Anny and I bring to ours. Though he is ten years younger than me, I know I have a lot to learn from him. For example, he is constantly reminding me to "turn to the kids" when I am most perplexed. That is essential, but I keep forgetting it.

Here is a letter that Fred wrote to his freshman students and passed along to me. Again, I like his effort to engage his students, in both the working out of his own dilemmas and the larger discussion going on in the school.

I keep thinking how nice it would be if you could read a

piece of literature and react to it critically, identify the artistry. But the real question is why. How important is getting excited about literature to you? I guess I should also be concentrating on making connections to your lives, revealing insights that are still viable. I did a little of this this year, but more might make the whole literature thing more relevant to all of us.

Part of my frustration comes from dealing with the canon: those books that the powers-that-be have determined I need to expose you to. And don't get me wrong, I don't have a problem with requiring you to read texts. I just don't know how to do it successfully.

If you noticed, I tried many different approaches throughout the year to get you guys through the books. Nothing really seemed to work. I assigned selections and quizzed you, I gave you the book a month before we began and asked you to have it finished in seven weeks, I covered the work in class, and I assigned you portions to teach your classmates. I guess the method that worked the best was asking you to lead the class. But time, man, time, there's never enough time. I get so overwhelmed by what I am supposed to cram into your brains that I feel pressure to come to closure quickly and move on. My biggest concern still is how to make sure everyone succeeds.

## Trying Readers' Workshop in the "Real World"

I was invited to speak to a group of student teachers at Loyola University of Chicago who were using my book *Situations* in class. Because I was still in the midst of trying to figure out what to do about reading, it wasn't long before I got off the topic of my book and began talking about reading workshops at the high-school level. A few months after that visit, I got call from one of the students, Mary Teising-Ruggiero, who was student teaching "low ability" students at a high school in Chicago. She had tried the novel *Lilies of the Field* with the kids, but it had been a dismal failure. "The kid's lack of attention," she later wrote, "their disinterest, rudeness, the poor attendance, and my initial student-teacher frustrations caused me to one day throw the entire thing out." She wanted to try reading workshop, so we talked it through and I sent her some of the daily reading response sheets I use. (See Appendix D.)

Mary wrote to me after that experience. I was impressed that so early in her career, she has such fine instincts: She clearly wants to connect with student interest and build her curriculum from there, but she also feels a responsibility to curricular demands; she is willing to take risks and is highly reflective in the process. She is demanding both of her students and of herself. As you read, remember that this is a twenty-two-year-old woman who has not yet been assigned her own classroom:

I noticed many different ability levels in my classes which logically told me that I couldn't teach all of my kids in the same way. This reality was overwhelming because I knew very little of the various methods to use or how to gear different techniques to different kids. That may be why *Lilies of the Field* felt like a total disaster. The readers' workshop idea seemed a way to deal with this concern.

I wanted to start out small, so I began with a unit on poetry in which my students chose their own poems to examine. I wanted to give them a sense of autonomy and ownership. This also gave me an opportunity to utilize the library. I had chosen and set out on a table about twenty books of poetry that I felt would be of interest to certain students considering their interests that I knew of. I didn't want to actually give these books to specific people in fear of being the one to choose for them. I told them these books were on the table if they were interested.

I was truly amazed by how the class' demeanor changed suddenly when we were in the library. I couldn't believe how quiet and seemingly intrigued they were while looking for their books. The librarian asked me what I had bribed them with.

I had been reading a lot of Louise M. Rosenblatt where she examines the reciprocal nature of the literary experience. She explains that meaning is neither "in" the text nor "in" the reader. She claims, and I agree, that "each reading is a particular event involving a particular reader and particular text under particular circumstances."

When I think back to when I was in school, I think that teachers too often unintentionally turned their students off to reading and extrapolating ideas because of the parameters, limits, rules, preconceived themes, etc., they imposed on our study of the book. Who's to say that my kids don't have a totally audacious but related idea about the reading that we never would have realized?

The poetry went well, so I initiated the workshop with short stories. We returned to the library to choose books. Two days after we started, only some of my students bought into the workshop. Some were more reticent about the idea; maybe not the idea so much as the freedom. This was all so foreign to them. Some kids found books right away, others looked for several days, a few filled out all the required response sheets in one day, and some slept the whole time. But one kid came to me for help and suggestions on what to read, a kid who had never spoken a positive word before! It was also really neat to see the kids write about their understanding of the books they chose!

## Defining the Question

I sent copies of some of these letters to my mentor, Susan Handler, who further refined my thinking with her response. I duplicated her letter for the department:

> The question of your letter to your department is: Should we allow kids to choose whatever books they want or should we demand that they read certain books that we believe are essential to becoming well educated?
>
> Actually, this debate has lost considerable weight for me. Why can't we do both? Perhaps there is something to be gained for reading a book together and sticking out a book that the kids wouldn't have chosen on their own. I already know there is a lot to be gained by giving kids choices in book selection. If we stay stuck at this point in the argument, we never need to address the more messy questions: What do the kids do when they read books, whether self-chosen or mandated? Which kids take off? Which remain on the outskirts of reading? Why? What kinds of interventions do I make as a teacher when I find some of the kids are not engaged? How do I decide what to do for each kid, recognizing there is no uniform right decision?
>
> I think it would be much simpler to argue whether Bloom or Atwell is correct. I think it's more difficult to acknowledge that teaching is very artistic, which means we make decisions about

our responses to and requirements of students in context. That means the decisions emerge from what is happening in that classroom, at that moment, coupled with what I need as a teacher to fulfill my beliefs about learning and what students need to learn.

No one has a prescription for this; it is too varied, too fluid. I'm certainly not opposed to the kids knowing some of the "significant" works. There is a wealth of tradition that can be used to stimulate thought and feeling. However, we need to find some way to give kids a strong sense that what they think and feel as they read is legitimate, important, and valid. I think we are looking for the bridge between the students' own reading and the body of works we would like them to read.

## The Transition to Boundary-Crossing Literature

### A Question of Timing

Along with David Denby (1996), I believe that "pleasure is the route to understanding; you expand on what you love, going from one enthusiasm to the next, one piece of music to the next, one book to the next, and finally what you end up with as the sum of these pleasures is your own soul" (75). But, again with Denby (and after some prodding from Anny), I have to wonder how (or if) "pleasure" alone will lead children to consider deeply concepts like *justice* and *happiness* (in the Platonic sense) not to mention a host of other ideals that the children of a democratic society ought to be grappling with.

I once had a middle-level senior class comprised mostly of African-American students—there were three white students and one from Iran. At the beginning of the year, they wanted to make it clear to me that, as one girl stated bluntly, "I don't read." The first book I tried with them, Richard Wright's *Native Son*, was initially a tough sell because of its length. ("Don't even tell me we're reading the whole thing!") But in time, and through a blend of cajoling, arm-twisting, and the promise that "the story will hook you," the kids did come around, did finish the book, and, in the end, decided on their own to reenact the trial of Bigger Thomas.

But the lack of racial diversity in the class made the selection of future readings an interesting challenge. They wanted more books like *Native Son*, books "that are real, that are about stuff we care about." My first instinct was to bring in more African-American writers, but now more and more a part of me keeps thinking that there are many books about "stuff' they could care about and not all are written by African-American writers. Not to expect my students to read more widely, I was beginning to believe, seemed like pandering. So, as a part of a larger unit on non-fiction, I assigned Elie Wiesel's *Night*, an affecting telling of his Nazi concentration camp experiences at the age of fourteen.

Three days into our study of the book, I started hearing complaints about how "boring" the book was and some harsh criticism of my decision to include it in our reading. "Not the Holocaust again!" In my eleven years as a teacher at ETHS, I've found that attention paid to the Holocaust can, and often does, draw to the surface some politically charged issues which manifest themselves in remarks like, "How come we don't spend this much time on slavery?" and "Why should we read about this when we don't even care?" Wiesel's autobiographical work treads on sensitive ground which I was disinclined to turn into a pedagogical or political battlefield. But our classroom, which Marvin Hoffman, in *Chasing Hellhounds* (1996), aptly refers to as "our fragile little skiff", hit very stormy, very angry seas. And I was left wondering, yet again, whether I was wrong to mandate what they would read. Was it possible I could jeopardize their taste for other literature by insisting too soon and too ardently that they expand their interest? I also had to wonder how they got to be seniors with so narrow a view, such limited experience.

Taking my cue from Fred, I decided to think this dilemma through in front of the kids. So, during our four-day Thanksgiving break, I wrote this letter, which I also distributed to the English Department and the administration:

> I woke up Thanksgiving morning thinking about our class. I was still hearing your complaints that *Night* was "boring," and your questions about why I would make you read it. "We already did the Holocaust," you said. "This is just another story we already heard." I thought about your comparison to *Native Son*. You said, "That was good. I could relate." One of you pointed to my copy of Luis J. Rodriguez' new book, *Always Running*, about gang life in L.A. and asked, "Why can't we read that?" Someone else said, "Why's everything we read in school have to be so *depressing*?" I'd heard all of this many times

before—believe me they are common complaints—but today I got to thinking about them.

I used to be shocked that anyone could be so callous as to find Wiesel's horrifying and painful experience "boring." I'd launch into the same old "blah-blah-blah" speech about the importance of knowing and understanding other cultures. But those responses didn't mean anything to me, today. And I'm beginning to understand why they may mean little to some of you.

Perhaps it's because we don't learn what we really need to learn about other cultures simply by being exposed to them. Watching ethnic dances at an assembly, sampling ethnic food at a "multi-cultural fair," or reading books written by "minorities" is a start, but only a start. Perhaps of more importance is our working *very* hard to discover the *universality* of the experiences described. The sufferings and indignities endured by real people like Elie Wiesel, Richard Wright, and Luis Rodriguez, and the troubles faced by fictional characters like Bigger Thomas and those in the books of Amy Tan, Toni Morrison, and Mark Twain, in some very basic way, belong to all of us. The pasts of all races in this country mingle. The histories of African-Americans and white Americans, for example, are inseparably intertwined. That's American history.

The specifics of our grief differ, of course, but literature is about *people*—people in difficult, demanding situations trying to find their way out of those situations, make sense of them, or simply to endure them. We don't have to have experienced the Holocaust or know someone who has or even admit we *care about* the Holocaust to want to know what happens when a person with an ardent faith in God (or an ardent faith in anything—family, humanity, himself) has that faith tested to its limits. You don't have to be Jewish to understand what it is like to be hated for one thing, like your religion or race. Literature *is* other people's stories, other people's troubles, and we read them (or watch them or listen to them) to help us understand our own stories. Knowing Elie Wiesel, Bigger Thomas, Luis Rodriguez will bring us closer to knowing ourselves and, on some deeper level, each other.

I am very happy, for example, that I didn't shut Malcolm X out of my own life simply because I am white and didn't have life experiences similar to his. I've read his autobiography a number of times because it teaches me about having the courage of my convictions even in the face of intense criticism and, perhaps more importantly, the courage to change when those convictions no longer hold up. For that reason alone, I'm grateful that Malcolm committed his story to paper.

Finally, in response to the complaint that literature is so often *depressing*, I'd like to quote Marvin Hoffman who, in his book *Chasing Hellhounds* (1996), reminds us that "most vital literature draws on the underside of human relationships and human emotions." But, he says, "in spite of the depressing subject matter, the books are often uplifting testimonials to the power of the human spirit to survive adversity and even be ennobled by it. An encounter with social and religious prejudices leaves a character not crushed but strong, and clearer about who he or she is" (141). Lastly, but perhaps most importantly, "stories reconnect us with one of the basic impulses to find within them some lessons for how to live our lives or how to make sense of what we have endured" (143).

I believe that it would be an insult to your intelligence if I only handed you material of immediate and high interest to you. You are more complex than that. Your abilities are limitless and so are your interests, even though you haven't yet discovered all of them. I think that it is part of my job, my responsibility to you, to introduce you to material you might not otherwise have encountered and to help you see what even a book about people living long ago and far away has to do with *your* life. Books, as Marv says, are not material to be "approached as a set of artifacts outside of yourselves, to be perused, analyzed, dismembered" (142). Rather, they are an invitation to explore how they interact with your life.

With all of this in mind, I was wondering what it would be like if, as we continued to work with *Night*, we thought about what we would want to read next that would increase our understanding of some aspect of the book—the testing of faith, the cruelty of racism, the power of the soul to somehow endure terrible hardship—that caught our interest, that connected with our lives? I'll offer suggestions of books I know about, and I'll count on you to do the same. We can see where our discussions lead us, always keeping an eye toward finding deeper ways to relate to, not only our own past, but the past of the human family.

We continued our reading. One student, Chris, who had been the first to ask, "Why are you making us read this?" drew an elaborate parallel between Jewish and African-American experience. Both were taken from their homes, he said, not told where they were going, and transported under cramped and terrible conditions. Upon arrival the dead were tossed aside, and the rest either sent to work or death. Families were cruelly divided "like they was puppies." When we finished the book, I asked my students to write a personal response to what we had read. The only "negative" comment came from a student who said, "I promised I'd read it, but I didn't promise I'd like it." Here are two other, more representative, responses:

> Mr. Larson, looking back, and how we was discouraged about reading *Night* and how we told you we already know about the Holocaust must have really broke your heart. When you wrote us that letter about why you want us to read the book you told us we all know something about the Holocaust, but we need to take the time to look at it from one person's point of view.
> It made me realize that I don't know enough about the hardship these people had to go through. Then slavery came into my mind, how other people of a different color control other people who may not look or think like them. Whites control blacks, Germans control Jews. I thought about how blacks was taken away from their family to do hard work for no pay. The same thing happened to the Jews and their families.
>                                   Tanya Esson

> This was a very sad and horrifying book to read. This book really touched my thoughts for white people. *Night* really made me think about all the pain a person can go through, regardless of race, creed, color, religion, etc. Slavery was a very painful time for black people so I can just imagine what it was like for the white man taking orders from another man just like himself. I will never forget the tragedy people in this world go through because of other people.
>                                   DeShauna Johnson

No other letter I wrote received as much response from students and faculty as this one. Colleagues came to me with materials, their thoughts, suggestions or just to say, "I've faced the same problem." I also received this fax from Marv Hoffman:

> Your Thanksgiving Day epistle to your students probes questions that are almost identical to those that have been at the heart of my own struggles as a classroom teacher. My torments, however, have been for the most part silent and internal, unprovoked by student protest.
>
> Here's the way it's looked to me. Faced with a class of never-tried-it readers, reluctant readers, and downright resisters, I've searched for the magical material that would unlock the reservoir of curiosity I've got to believe is waiting to be tapped in every human being. These are mostly African-American students, so I've gone to works like August Wilson's *Fences*, or, in a historical stretch, Frederick Douglass' autobiography. For kids as yet unconvinced that books represent anything in their lives, I've argued (silently), we can't move forward until the link is established.
>
> But literature has a second, perhaps greater purpose: to take us beyond ourselves, to enable us, as Atticus Finch tells his children, to walk in another man's shoes. If men are unable to see the world as women do or straights as gays, we are more likely to treat them as "others," leaving the door open for all manner of cruelty and callousness.
>
> The question becomes one of timing. When do we make the transition from the particular to the universal? When is the time right to shift from Douglass to Shakespeare, from *Fences* to Faulkner? This is where I have faltered. I've clung to the more recognizable, remained within my student's—and my own—comfort zone too long. Hey, the kids are reading, even appearing to enjoy it, why ruin a good thing?
>
> There are times when I think that I and teachers like me have come up short on the courage to break out of that comfort zone as you have with the introduction of *Night*. And look at the thinking, feeling, and learning that's emerged from that decision! As you point out, it would be downright condescending of you not to attempt to propel them beyond their particularity. You've prodded me to be braver about the timing of my transition to the boundary-crossing literature.
>
> And yet, and yet I have to sound a cautionary signal. A few

weeks ago, I heard a talk by Julius Lester, whose writings about slavery and the Black experience I admire and use in my classroom. He was recounting his schooling at Fisk University in the fifties, in which the existence of Black literature was barely acknowledged. His intellectual mother's milk was the classics and he thought he was a better man for it, one who saw no distinctions between Black suffering and laughter and that of others. This multi-cultural stuff was driving wedges between us, he argued.

What made me uncomfortable in the midst of the almost entirely white audience he was addressing was the fear that he was giving them permission to pass over that first step with their students of color, the one aimed at first convincing them that books have a place in their lives because their lives have a place in books.

What's amazing and wondrous about teaching, Mark, is the way in which every seemingly petty decision like the choice of what to read next opens out onto the most pressing and compelling political and philosophical issues. The classroom, viewed thoughtfully, is our own Yoknapatawpha County, that narrow sliver of the world that is in fact the world in miniature.

## Where My Thinking Has Brought Me

Peter Elbow, in *Embracing Contraries*, articulated the balance I'd like to strike: "In order to teach well," he says, "we must find *some* way to be loyal both to students and to knowledge or society. Any way we can pull it off is fine." That balance is hard to strike because of, as Elbow says, "the natural tendency of these two loyalties to conflict with each other (1986, 158).

I see my own career so far as one big swing of the pendulum from absolute loyalty to one to absolute loyalty to the other. I know I love to see my kids reading what they've found on their own and truly enjoying their choices, I love it when they talk to each other and to me about what they've read, and I love seeing them go out in search of books they've heard about. But I also love hearing students, even years after graduation, referring to some of our greatest literature, books they tell me they never would have picked up on their own. I get pangs when I look into classrooms where all the kids have the same book on their desk and the teacher is leading a discussion of, say, Holden's alienation. The scene is so comfortingly familiar, I miss it.

So for now, I'll keep striving to respond to Elbow's challenge to be loyal to students *and* to knowledge (or, in this context, the canon). I'll keep my eye on the great works of the past, while watching for ways to bridge them with students' particular interests. I'll also work to meet Susan's challenge to "give kids a strong sense that what they think and feel as they read is legitimate, important, and valid." And, perhaps most importantly, I'll continue to search for ways to be responsive to the kids' request for a chance to *see* the books we read, whatever we decide to read, through their own eyes. I think that Elbow may well be right: however we pull that off is fine.

## Books I Wish I'd Known About at the Time

*Joining the Literacy Club*, Frank Smith
*Literature as Exploration*, Louise M. Rosenblatt
*Literature Circles*, Harvey Daniels
*Great Books*, David Denby
*Ruined by Reading*, Lynn Sharon Schwartz

# Chapter Six

# Assessment

*Error marks the place where education begins.*
Mike Rose

All in all, things seemed to be going very well in the classroom. The kids and I were getting along, and they liked what we were doing. I would hear from students in other classes that they had heard what we were up to. They wanted to hear more. Was it possible I was finally learning how to teach? There were days when I practically bounded through the halls, cheerily greeting every person I passed. But all the while I had to wonder, how long would this last?

Not long. It would end with a question posed by a student named Lisa.

I had moved away from giving wholly open-ended writing assignments like "write three essays on what you care about." Conversations with Fred and Anny, among others, had persuaded me that kids needed more direction. But I still wanted to give them as much choice as possible. I was still very interested in helping them see their world as a place filled with writing possibilities, if they could just learn where and how to look. But until I got better at that, I gave my students a list of essay types (personal narrative, movie review, literary criticism—the usual list) and plied them with examples of these types of writing. Each day, after I showed them an example essay, I'd have them free-write for ten minutes. Some of those free-writes would later develop into finished drafts, others would just be filed away. The kids decided which essays they wanted to bring to completion. By the end of the semester, I expected them to have a *completed* example of each type on the list. I gave them a checklist so they could keep track. I also expected them to read at least one book from each of these categories:

Novel written before 1945
Novel written between 1945 and 1970
A current work of fiction or nonfiction
A play
A book of poetry
An extended news article
Two book reviews
Two movie or play reviews

When students finished reading one of these works, they filled out a Reading Response Sheet and arranged for a conference with me. Those reading conferences, incidentally, became one of the great pleasures of this job. I loved hearing the kids talk excitedly and with disarming insight about books they had selected and enjoyed. But I was still amazed by how many upperclassmen confessed, "This is the first time I read a whole book."

I conducted most class sessions like Nancie Atwell's workshops: mini-lesson followed by independent work. This way I was able to combine individual work and one-on-one instruction with whole-group discussions, which my students and I did enjoy. The kids worked on their essays in class and at home but in whatever order they chose. If they'd just seen a movie they liked or hated, for example, they might do the movie review next. If they needed to see more examples of completed works, I had a looseleaf notebook with samples both of published and student writing available to them.

I placed students in charge of their time as much as possible, then had them write progress reports every two weeks. (See Appendix E.) At the end of the year, they proposed a grade in writing, backing it up with evidence from their portfolio. I received many letters like this one from Kate Fiffer, a senior:

It was almost overwhelming how much freedom you gave us. The responsibilities that came along with the freedom were shocking and took some getting used to, but they were responsibilities that I needed in order to learn how to handle them. Because of this class, I have become more focused on what I personally want to learn, and I am learning simply because I want to instead of because that's what I'm supposed to be doing.

I don't want to lose everything I've gained in English this year. I hope that in the future, in English classes and in life, I can continue to have this feeling—a love of writing, a need to write in order to clear my thoughts, and a positive, excited attitude about learning.

I want to be in an atmosphere where I feel like it's OK, it's not wrong, to have made a mistake. I want to continue learning, not from a textbook or by a strict structure and grades, but because of the inner motivation I've reached.

Many more kids than ever before were engaged in their work. They were reading, they were writing, they were excited about what they were doing. So there I was, giddily skipping through the halls with a basket on my arm, tossing petals of pedagogical wisdom into the paths of teachers I passed.

Then Lisa nailed me. She arrived at my desk for a final-grade conference empty-handed.

"Where's your portfolio, where's your grade proposal letter?" I asked.

"How can I tell you what grade I earned?" she said. "I don't know what the standard is." She crossed her arms and stared. "What is the criterion for an A?"

I couldn't answer her. Cornered, I employed a time-honored teaching technique: turning my own bafflement into a learning experience for the student.

"Well, what do you think the standard is?"

But she was quick. "I have no idea," she said, eyes narrowed.

I felt myself slipping back into my old ways and was helpless to stop it. Just keep talking, I thought, she'll either lose interest or assume she's missing the point. I said that the standard had to be different for each student, in fact, for each paper each student wrote. The standard, for example, for a personal essay differs from the standard for a poem. It all has to do with what you are trying to accomplish with your essay. Audience and purpose. *Blah, blah, blah.* It had all sounded so good on paper and at workshops. But today, face to face with Lisa, I wasn't even convincing myself.

"You see?" I said, turning my eyes to the leaning stack of portfolios on my desk.

"No," she said. "Aren't there good poems and bad poems? Aren't

there good personal essays and bad personal essays? Or is it all"—
here she used her fingers to indicate quotation marks—'relative'?"
Then she couldn't resist a roll of the eyes.

What *did* a "finished" paper look like, I wondered? How *had* I
decided when to stamp each paper *completed*? And what *did* an A
portfolio look like? Surely, it couldn't just be a portfolio in which all
tasks were completed. That would take me back to the task lists I
was trying to avoid. And when I looked over those reading journals
and response sheets, how did I really know how well, how deeply a
student had read? Most of that judgment, I realized, was formed during my reading conferences with them. Shouldn't there be more con-
crete, more specific proof of their understanding? It must have something to do with the level of proficiency the student had achieved in
various areas. But how to measure that in a way that made sense,
was fair, meant something?

I had read articles and books on assessments. I had dug up district goals, both ours and those of other schools. Everything I read
provided strong, solid, valid rubrics that I tried to adapt for the purposes of my class. But few of those rubrics held up very long when
applied to actual portfolios. There was always another student or
another paper that was excellent for some indefinable, gut-level reason but that didn't fit the rubric; in fact, I often found that some of
the best writing didn't fit the criterion at all, and some of the bland-
est fit it perfectly. Of course, phony assessments were easy to find.
Giving points for "freedom from mechanical errors" or "organization" had always seemed, though comfortingly specific and familiar,
ultimately limited and limiting. Surely, good writing had to do with
more than just mechanical correctness, solid organization, and
focus. It also had to do with originality of thought and presentation,
vividness of language, precision, complexity of thought, ability to
reach, to move the audience. But how to measure that? And how to
place those values on some sort of scale that could be applied to all
students' work? The questions kept coming. And all the while that
one nagging question, "Can it be done?" which sometimes meta-
morphosed into, "Should it be done?"

When I looked up from the stack of files on my desk, I found that
Lisa had not broken her stare, but now she shifted in her seat. She
wanted the conversation to end. Clearly, I was unprepared to answer
her question. "If you can't tell me what the standard is," she said, "I
can't tell you what I earned."

Quite true.

She demanded that I decide on a grade for her since I was the one who was able to discern a measure for all this chaos.

Now what?

## In Search of Reliable Rubrics

Fortunately, it was the end of the year. The following September, Larry Geni, a science teacher, and I put a notice in the daily bulletin inviting interested teachers to attend an informal gathering every two weeks after school to talk through assessment techniques. Those talks were helpful to our articulating the problems and as a chance for experimenting teachers to commiserate, but specific, viable solutions remained outside our grasp. I also turned to my English colleagues and tried to open a conversation about the ways in which we assess students' learning and acquisition of skills. This is a letter I wrote to a member of the English Department after a conversation we'd had about assessments. Here, I am trying to get at what it is I want to evaluate, which I thought was a good place to start.

> It fascinates me that, when you consider how long there have been schools, we still don't know how to reliably and meaningfully assess what kids have learned and can do. It's an intriguing question, don't you think? Why does a valid and reliable rubric continue to elude us? Why isn't there some simple, specific, dependable standard for writing and reading that can be xeroxed and distributed to every teacher in America? There has to be a reason that every time we come up with one, we eventually toss it out.
>
> This is what I'm thinking: I used to treat reading and writing as tasks to be completed. At the end of the semester, I tallied up what students had done and didn't do and arrived at an average grade for all the work. But now I see reading and writing as skills, not tasks to be completed. Like any other skills, reading and writing require practice—trial and error, repetition, and an opportunity for each student to find which means and methods best suit him or her. I am looking for ways to shift the method of my courses away from a series of tasks to be competed, then evaluated, and move toward a way to let kids practice and hone

these two essential skills in their own way. They should have no fear of repercussions for an ill-fated but well-intentioned experiment. (Isn't that how we learned to teach, which is another skill?) Imagine learning to play the piano if each missed note resulted in a point being deducted. How could anyone practice, much less explore and experiment under those conditions? How could a unique style emerge? What would happen to joy and pleasure, which I believe are essential to engagement, perhaps the most important element of true and lasting learning.

So if I'm teaching skills, the time will come when I will need to evaluate the level of proficiency at which students are able to use these skills. I try to test their ability to read and to react to what they read in writing, and to write effectively for different audiences and different purposes. I think I have found satisfactory ways of getting them to do those things. But I have no idea how to assess it. What are your thoughts?

Then Anny wrote:

"TO: English teachers en masse, and others interested in curriculum. RE: Mark's continuing effort to examine all assumptions."

I believe that the department needs to clarify, mainly for the sake of the students' continual growth, our direction regarding reading, writing, and evaluation. During the course of our discussions, we may find that there are multiple directions, perhaps for different grade levels, ability levels, or just individual idiosyncracities. I am comfortable with teachers being themselves and am very grateful that ETHS has demonstrated a high level of tolerance for individualism. I have seen, over and over again, that all teachers do best when dealing with subjects they love. No matter what else we gain or lose, that freedom is very important to me.

That said, I think students need clarification about the extent to which different standards are necessary in a department of strong individuals, and the extent to which we all agree on some basics. There must be some bottom line from which we can work. What books will students read, what constitutes an excellent paper, etc.? This is something we can and certainly ought to do.

I responded publicly to Anny's letter:

> I'd like to speak my mind on your feeling that we need very specific and high expectations for students' writing. Of course we do, who would argue with that? But, in my classes we discover that there are many ways of articulating thought. Right now, rather than impress a single standard on students, my impulse is to start with what he has in writing and try to discover where he wants to go with it. Then, together, we can try to get there. It's a fascinating game of investigation and discovery.
>
> Form (did I make this up?) follows function. Tell me what you intended to do with this essay—who is your audience and what is your purpose—and then we'll talk about whether and to what degree you were successful. This becomes a good moment to talk and think about specific matters of form.
>
> I am in the process of putting together a looseleaf notebook in which I am collecting examples of what I consider high-quality writing by students and published authors. It is a useful tool. I can say, "Look how this author dealt with a similar problem" or, "How does your movie review compare to this one?" Perhaps that's where the standards should be, in examples, rather than in easily measured but not particularly revealing rubrics.

## Raising Questions About Current Tests

It seemed to me that the inquiry into what we really wanted to assess and how we would assess it was hampered by some of the evaluation methods and devices we already had in place. Two tests in particular bothered me more each year I had to face them: the Language Proficiency Test (grammar) and the Writing Competency Test. I felt they not only didn't achieve their desired ends, but were actually counterproductive. I agreed with Bill Ayers who argues that the danger of such tests is that they "push well-intentioned teachers and school leaders in the wrong direction; they constrain teachers' energies and minds, dictating a disastrously narrow range of activities and experiences, and offering little help in the important job of figuring out where kids are in order to present the next challenge" (1993, 118).

But both of these tests had been in place at our school for many years and their efficacy was assumed. Raising questions about these tests would prove a more ticklish matter than I expected. Some teachers actually resented my suggestion that we reexamine them, calling my letters "divisive." Such strong reaction only confirmed my feeling that these tests warranted a second look.

## The Grammar Test

Our Language Proficiency Test has been administered to all grades at ETHS since 1975. A lot of time and money went into developing the twelve different exams, one for every ability level within each grade. Each test consists of one-hundred items. No two teachers prepare for the test in the same way. Some do a little grammar work every week throughout the year. Some set aside three or four weeks just before the exam. Some do nothing at all. About four years ago, I abandoned preparation for this exam. I just gave my kids the test; if they wanted to see the results, I showed them. I didn't record the grade. Although I never felt completely at ease with this, I felt worse about spending any class time on these isolated grammar skills. Two teachers once did an experiment. They compared the grades students received the year they prepared the class for the tests to the grades students received when the teachers did no preparation. They saw no difference.

I decided to take the senior honors test myself to see what it was like. I ran my test through the Scan-Tron machine and, I must tell you, I was startled when I saw the score. I wrote the following to the department the next day:

I took the senior honors Language Proficiency Test yesterday. I got a 67, a C-. How should I feel about this? What does my 67 mean? What does it say about me as a teacher, a writer, as an educated person?

I suppose I could have studied for the test. Drilled myself. Done some exercises in the grammar book. I even could have asked colleagues to clarify what I didn't understand. It might have been interesting to see what I could get if I prepared. Maybe I could have gotten a 100. But what would *that* mean?

I was pondering these questions when I got a call from a

friend who teaches at a nearby high school. When I asked him what sort of annual grammar test they give, he said, "We don't have anything like that. You *do?*" Then he asked the tough question: "Why?"

A solid working knowledge of our language and its many variations is crucial. I agree with Lisa Delpit who, in *Other People's Children*, rightly insists that all students must be taught "the codes needed to participate fully in the mainstream of American life" (45) (ie., standard English). To expect anything less of ourselves is a gross disservice to our students. I never have and never will argue against "mastery" of our language. But I can't see how this test and the preparation it necessitates serve that end.

Delpit says that learning to speak (and, presumably, to write) a form of language that is different from one's own "is not principally a function of cognitive analysis, thereby not ideally learned from protracted rule-based instruction and correction. Rather, it comes from exposure, comfort level, familiarity, and practice in real communicative contexts" (49). Maybe these four strategies deserve our attention. I don't see how grammar exercises and our present test fit with any of these possibilities.

It seems to me that there are certain aspects of written and oral language (a. that, b. which) are essential for students to learn and be able to employ with ease. The list probably isn't very long. Certainly not long enough to fill twelve one-hundred item tests. What would we come up with if we tried to arrive at some agreement on a list of those essentials? Once we produced such a list, we could all focus on those matters each year. What do we stand to lose that isn't already lost to bewildering minutia? We've said it many times: The kids often forget even the simplest points of grammar from year to year. We ought to ask, "Why?"

## The Writing "Competency" Test

Freshmen and junior students are given a ninety-minute period in which to write on a topic they have not seen in advance. The topics themselves are usually pretty dry: "What three qualities do you look for in a friend?" or "What three qualities make a good teacher?" Students are expected to respond to these questions in specifically structured essays. There is one acceptable format only: The essay must have a clear topic sentence, three supporting arguments with elaboration, effective transitions, and a sound conclusion. The papers are expected to be reasonably free of mechanical errors and to follow strict manuscript form (written in black ink and only on one side of the paper, with a correctly placed title and one-inch margins). Students are penalized for having less than three supporting arguments. They must also choose one side of the issue. The more complex the question, the more difficult that can be, especially for the kids who see multiple dimensions in an issue. For example, a recent question was, "Write about three reasons why living near Chicago is either a benefit or a problem." One of my students asked me, "What if I consider it both a problem and a benefit?" I had to say, "Choose one." I believe that although the test may be helpful in preparing students for a state-mandated writing test, its usefulness as a reliable measure of writing "competency" has waned. Its primary virtue is its use as a sorting tool, telling us which kids will need remedial help in writing the following year and which won't. However, by the time the test is given in March, any teacher could easily prepare a list of those kids.

My concern is that preparation for the Writing Competency Test distorts our teaching of writing, forcing us to drill kids on this singular format when we could be helping them explore the wide array of organizational patterns competent writers find for putting their complex thoughts into words. I should think that good writing has more to do with the clear and interesting articulation of solid thinking than it does with the reproduction of some orthodox form. Yet our highest marks tend to go to students who perform the latter proficiently, irrespective of the quality of their thinking. My other concern is that the implicit message in any test is that what we are testing for is what we value. Students reasonably get the message, no matter what we actually say, that this is the type of writing we value and these are the qualities we value in their writing.

I once gave myself ninety minutes to write an essay on "Three Reasons Why I Can't Take This Test." I found the highly specific organizational pattern surprisingly difficult to work with. What I wanted to say was constantly at odds with the format. But I distributed what I wrote to the English faculty. One teacher said, "I get your point, but I have to tell you the writing isn't nearly as good as some of your other stuff." I thought, "Then you missed my point."

Admittedly, however, the tone of the essay was cynical; appropriately, the response I received from the English Department was negative. Fred handled his concerns about the test in a different and, I think, more constructive way. Where I had angrily belittled the test, Fred again opened a discussion with his students about his own thoughts on the test and invited them to submit theirs to the department office.

> I love writing. I love when you love writing. Writing, for me, is discovery and expression; it's also memos, grocery lists, Valentine's Day cards. It would be (in the most un-Holden sense of the word) grand if you could all write to discover and express. But, alas, there is more to writing than that. And as your English teacher, I feel a sense of responsibility to prepare you for writing you will be doing in college and in the workplace. In that sense, I believe the writing that I have you do must reflect real writing you will be doing.
>
> "Back in the day" when I was in college, the writing I did was expository, persuasive, and analytic. You should be able to do those types when you interface your brain with a piece of college-ruled paper. I think it is also important that the assignments I have you do are set in a meaningful context. One thing I feel I need to teach you is that these formatting techniques you are asked to demonstrate on competency tests are not only structures but strategies. Once you have mastered cookbook formulaic formats, however, you need to bust out and fly. You need to know that your writing has the potential to be dynamic, and not static.

Fred then challenged his students to write a letter to the English Department explaining how they felt about the test: "How do you think it assesses your abilities as a writer? How well does it model writing you have done in the past? How well does it anticipate writing you may do in the future?"

He warned them that change in an institution happens slowly and that if their thoughts did bring about change it would be evident "farther up the road." In the meantime, he told them, "If your suggestion is used or even talked about in the English Department, I'll write you a personal check for twenty-five dollars."

I responded to Fred that same day:

I was so excited by your note to your kids that I had to hit the keys immediately. I'll bet some of the kids will do the same. What a gift you have given them: an opportunity to fight back on paper—an authentic purpose.

I loved your enthusiasm for writing coupled with a pragmatic concern for what lay ahead. But Fred, where are your three supports? Also, I don't remember seeing *alas* on the list of transition words. And do you call "I'll write you a check for twenty-five dollars" a sound conclusion?

After taking the writing competency test, one of my students said he could only come up with one reason to support his thesis. But, he said, it was a really good one. Couldn't he just talk about that? I had to say that the evaluators would not look upon it kindly. So he wrote about the one solid reason he had. "After that," he later said, "I was talking through my butt." I'm disinclined to unravel that metaphor, but I have a pretty good idea what it means. I think we demanded that he write that way.

You make an excellent distinction between structures and strategies. I hadn't thought in those terms before. You tell the kids that once they have mastered formulaic formats they "need to bust out and fly." For some, I would think, that will work. For others, I wonder if it isn't the reverse. (Or is every kid the same?) I should think a dancer needs to see what his body can do before he learns a specific dance. Ideally, our kids would have been doing some romping on paper before they come to us. But my own twelve-year-old twins have been writing these formulaic papers for several years now with rare opportunity to write something creative, interesting, and meaningful to them. Their teachers tell me they're getting students ready for high school. High school says they're getting kids ready for state tests. Who's teaching them to write as a way of thinking, of communicating complex ideas, of expressing our deepest longings and most ardent wishes?

I'd hate to think that we are employed to teach kids to write via butt.

Today, two years after Fred wrote his note and made his offer, the debate about the value of that test persists, and so does the test itself. Fred has been able to hang on to his twenty-five dollars.

## Minority Student Achievement

Nowhere, at least at my school, is the question of assessment more in need of a good hard look than in the way it affects the schooling of minority students. We are frustrated because we see the necessity of acting swiftly and surely, and yet we really don't know how to proceed.

What we know, in fact, is not much. We know that minority students tend, as a group, to perform less well on standardized tests and in many of our classrooms. We know that, as a result, there is a sharp disparity between the racial makeup of our honors classes and the lower-level classes.

Because our understanding of the problem is slight and, at times wrong-headed, our solutions tend to be short-lived efforts. For example, one year the board mandated that every department develop a strategy to deal with the problem. We were given several months. The English Department landed on an idea we called "Focus on Five." We'd each "target" five minority students whom we felt needed special attention and then we'd, well, focus on them. We'd make a point of scheduling frequent meetings between ourselves and the students. We'd keep track of their absences, tardies, quiz and test scores, and the frequency with which the chosen five did their homework. We hoped that these data would reveal that increased attention led to academic achievement. It's not a terrible idea, but it only responds to a small part of the issue, and I was uncomfortable with the way it forced us to identify five kids, minority kids at that, who looked to us like potential failures.

But, most destructively, I thought, the plan had the same effect as the grammar and writing tests: It led us astray and freed us, albeit temporarily, from looking more deeply at this complex problem. And so the issue would go unaddressed, at least in any meaningful way, for another year.

## Seeing with Fresh Eyes

I kept thinking we should try looking at the problem from a different angle. Our "solutions" tended always to be larger or more intensified versions of what we already were doing. We needed a "plan" to get us to pay closer attention to our students? Lisa Delpit *in Other People's Children* had already convinced me that it's really not new reform programs and ideas we lack, but "basic understandings of who we are and how we are connected to and disconnected from one another" (xv). She believes that

> . . . the best solutions will arise from the acceptance that alternative world views exist [. . .] We all interpret behaviors, information, and situations through our own cultural lenses; these lenses operate involuntarily, below the level of conscious awareness, making it seem that our view is simply "the way it is." [. . .] We must consciously and voluntarily make our cultural lenses apparent. Engaging in the hard work of seeing the world as others see it must be a fundamental goal for any move to reform the education of teachers and their assessment (151).

These basic understandings are essential because, as Delpit points out, "when teachers do not understand the potential of the students they teach, they will under-teach them no matter what the methodology" (175). It seemed to me that most of our plans addressed students' weaknesses, or what we perceived to be their weaknesses. I wondered what it would be like if we were forced to identify and teach to their strengths? I wrote the following letter with the hope of giving us a different way of looking at the same problem:

> I've just finished reading Mike Rose's *Lives on the Boundary*, which I think is extremely important to our discussion of (minority) student achievement. He advocates "talking through the places where new knowledge clashes with ingrained beliefs" (194). I understand why we are in a hurry to arrive at solutions. But I don't think we can escape the need to learn how to challenge our assumptions about our students and how they learn *while* we continue to devise immediate action.
>
> Here's an eye-opener, always a good way to start: In the chapter "Crossing Boundaries," Rose lays out the origins of the notion of remedial education, an understanding of which, I think, is invaluable to understanding our present actions—why we do what we do the way we do it.
>
> The word *remedial* originated in the nineteenth century in medicine and law. It referred to persons with neurological problems. *Remedial* has its root (both in etymology and intent) in the word *remedy*. When used in education circles, the word

quickly generalized to mean everything from special educational needs to problematic home lives. But the medical attitude, Rose points out, remained. Educators tried (continue to try) to diagnose disabilities and then to remedy them. People thought (think) in terms of corrective teaching. "Then they set out to diagnose as precisely as possible the errors (defects) in a student's paper [. . .] and designed drills and exercises to remedy them" (210).

Rose argues, and I would too, that we are still entrapped by this view of students and learning. Students who don't perform well on our tests or cannot—or refuse to—perform our "constrained and ordered tasks" are treated as if they have a disease. They are "forced to sit in scholastic quarantine until their disease can be diagnosed and remedied" (210). Ironically, this often isolates them from exposure to and contact with that which we will continue to punish them for not understanding: "the shared concepts and catch phrases, nuances and references of Western thinking" (194)—that which can best be attained through immersion. I suggest that we will remain entrapped until we begin to talk our way out.

Rose, condemning America's belief that "to measure is to initiate a cure," offers this caution: "A focus on quantification—on errors we can count, on test scores we can rank-order—can divert us from rather than guide us toward solutions. Numbers seduce us into thinking we know more than we do; they give the false assurance of rigor, but reveal little about the complex cognitive and emotional processes behind the tally of errors and wrong answers" (200).

Rose suggests we seek to discover the "intelligence of a student's mistake" (172). "Before we shake our heads at these errors, we should consider the possibility that many [. . .] linguistic bungles are signs of growth, a stretching beyond what [students] can comfortably do with [for example] written language" (188).

## Where I've Come in My Thinking

I'm sorry to say that I'm still unable to reply as well as I would like to Lisa, my skeptical student, who asked, "What is the standard?" I'm getting closer, but I'm still searching for more sophisticated, specific and reliable means of measuring competency, skill, and success.

I was recently on a panel charged with selecting several exemplary teachers from more than eight-hundred to win a prestigious award for the quality of their teaching. The screening and evaluation process provided some interesting possibilities for how we might score students' work.

In the awards' selection process, each applicant submits several essays and letters of recommendation. These writings are first read by a team of two educators. They each secretly write down a score for the essays, then share their scores with each other. If they agree, the writings are passed on to another pair, who repeat the same process. If they disagree, either with each other or the previous readers, they talk out their differences until they agree on a summary score. Applicants with low scores are eliminated. The process continues involving more readers, more exacting evaluation, and more elimination until the final winners are finally selected.

I learned a lot about teaching while I was on that panel. Because there was no highly specific rubric for what makes an excellent teacher, I found that each application and each ensuing discussion with my partners redefined my notion, each added a new facet to my thinking and enriched my understanding of teaching. My definition of excellence remained in flux, not because it was equivocal but because it was growing, developing.

The process made me wonder what it would be like for all teachers periodically to look at several student essays or, for that matter, portfolios, in the same way. Peter Elbow argues that "one of the main reasons why evaluation of writing is so problematic is that the model of evaluation used is at odds with the thing being evaluated." He goes on to say that teachers tend to emphasize features they can easily agree upon, like grammar and spelling, or they "set up oversimple models of good writing such as the 'five-paragraph essay' because graders can spot and agree on deviations from it. But, says Elbow, "when the thing being evaluated is a complex human performance like writing [or, as in the previous example teaching], the most natural model for trustworthy evaluation is not one evaluative verdict but a small array of perceptions." (1986, 224).

And yet, more and more I agree with Anny that we, as a department, ought to create common expectations. But, so far, that has been difficult. Anny, Fred, and another teacher, Warren, and I have begun to work at coming to some agreement in our expectations for written work. If a student transferred from my class to Anny's—even though our points of view are often dissimilar—the expectations for writing would be clear to the student. We plan to meet periodically and grade papers together to refine our assessment.

The conversations that our work on this project have so far generated are fascinating. For example, I feel that impact should be part of the evaluation. Fred and Anny believe that because it is so difficult to measure, it should not be included. I say that most of what students will face as adults will be ambiguous. Is that a "good" movie, book, political candidate, sales pitch? Anny says that writing is about technique; I say that technique ultimately serves impact. Fred says he wants to be able to tell a student exactly why a paper doesn't work. . . .

And so the debate goes on. As it should. In fact, I would like next to see us engage in this conversation as a department and for the dialogue to be ongoing. Whatever we decide and however we make that decision, I hope that we will be primarily guided not by what is easiest or most expedient for us, but by what best serves the needs of the students.

## Books I Wish I'd Known About at the Time

*The Language Instinct*, Steven Pinker
*Measuring Up*, Robert Rothman
*Assessing Student Performance*, Grant Wiggins
*Punished by Rewards*, Alfie Kohn

# Introduction to Part III

# Conversations with Students
## An Evolving Challenge

*Teaching is an interactive practice that begins and ends with seeing the student. This is more complicated than it seems, for it is something that is ongoing and never completely finished. The student grows and changes, the teacher learns, the situation shifts, and seeing becomes an evolving challenge.*

William Ayers

Gretchen, a senior, stood at my desk less than a week before research papers were due and said, "I don't think I'm going to finish my paper in time. I've had a very bad weekend."

How many times had I heard about bad weekends? I said, "So what happened?"

"A close friend died. A car crash. Haven't you heard?"

I'm still annoyed but also amazed and intrigued by how my old impulses as a teacher continue to thrive. My first reaction to Gretchen's words was not sympathy or concern. My first reaction, I'm ashamed to say, was skepticism. How convenient, I thought.

"I haven't heard," I said. "What can you tell me?"

She explained how she and a large number of friends had been at a party, how after the party two cars drove side by side, too fast and too close for the icy street. One driver, a former student of mine, lost control, jumped the curb, and slammed into a tree. She was saved by an airbag. Steven, in the passenger's seat, died instantly.

The class found their seats behind Gretchen as she talked to me. I sat with them and said nothing for some moments. This usually animated and noisy room was dark and still. Finally, I asked, "How's everybody doing? Are you OK?"

First, more silence. Then sniffles, tears, a few heads lowered.

I said, "Do you want to talk about it?"

Slowly, they did. They talked of their anger, their pain, their stunned amazement at the suddenness and permanence of what happened. We would talk about Steve for several more days. His death and our response to it did not replace the curriculum, it became the curriculum. *Slaughterhouse-Five* and the research paper, I decided, would have to wait.

At the end of the third day, however, I said we'd have to face the matter of the book and the paper. We had to make some decisions. The kids were silent. I tried prompting them. "What do you need? What do you suggest?" They had become quite good at telling me what they needed and wanted. But today it was too much to ask. So I voiced what I had suspected was the problem: "Are you having trouble asking for an extension?"

Jessica said, "I feel like we'd be using Steve's death as an excuse—almost like his death was the answer to our prayers, at least as far as the paper is concerned."

"Of course we want more time," said Katie, who had been in the second car. "But I don't want to feel like Steve paid for it."

I said, "What if I give you permission to postpone the paper? Unfortunately, things like this happen. Life can't come to a halt, but we can't deny that it's been altered, either."

The kids then spent a day devising an alternate schedule.

As the week progressed, I was startled by the conversation I heard among some faculty members. Of course, most teachers grieved with their students. We had lost a child. But a few said things that disturbed me, perhaps because these were some of my own unspoken thoughts. Some teachers were peeved, for example, because Steve's funeral was held during the school day. He hadn't been an exemplary student; in fact, he was often at odds with school. A relative thought he would appreciate the idea of his classmates getting out of class for him. One teacher said, "If his friends care that much about him, they can just as easily go after school." Several other teachers felt that this decision opened the door for students who didn't even know Steve to get out of class. And then there was the matter of his known drug and alcohol use and speculation that it played a part in the crash. I heard, "We don't want to glorify that! Suddenly, this kid's a hero!"

Students, meanwhile, had begun to write about Steve. We put those writings on the bulletin board along with a *Chicago Tribune* article about the accident. One girl, Sarah, who didn't know Steve, put up a poem that had been written a few years earlier by another student after one of our kids was murdered at a party. Sarah said the poem articulated "exactly how I feel."

> She didn't cry for the loss of a friend
> They had never laughed together
> or talked together.
> She cried for the loss other people felt
> Those who had laughed together and talked together with him.
> They now walked silent
> with pain in their eyes
> as if a word would destroy
> the last piece of life
> they still believed in.

One night, I went to the place where the accident occurred. It was a horrifying scene: a huge, uprooted tree; a mangled fence; two deep, muddy trenches in the grass where the tires failed to find their grip. And nearby was a circle of candles and mementos the kids had placed there. I came home and wrote the following for my students. I later learned that this piece was placed, with the other mementos, on the scene.

I visited the place where Steven left you. You have lighted the spot, a small oval, with candles, defined it with a garland of flowers. Letters, photographs and poems, cigarettes, a stuffed animal. The memories are earthbound; to make certain, you have stabbed them with pencils, afraid they'll lift and leave. Nearby, a fallen tree, torn from the ground, but magnificently iced, as if strung with a thousand tiny lights.

The tree will be removed, the mementos will fly. But that is as it should be. Steve isn't there. What remains now travels with you. And I pray that Katy will be right, that Steve's dying will save many lives—yours and each life you touch, as you move farther and farther away from the place where Steven left you.

I attended Steve's funeral—I had cut class, too—and when I witnessed my students' agony, I was ashamed all over again by my initial reaction—"how convenient"—even though, I hope, it never manifested itself in any way.

But it made me think. And it made me ask, "Is school that separate from the lives of our students that real life must compete with it for their attention? Shouldn't school be a place where we learn to make sense of life?"

I wonder still whether I was wrong to have postponed the research paper or to have put our work on hold for so long while we talked about Steve. A teacher I admire for a variety of reasons said that the kids have to learn that life goes on, so he didn't alter his schedule. Should I have done that too? I don't know. I also worry that I may have acted outside my expertise when I asked my students if they wanted to talk. And maybe I'm being unfair to be so critical of my skeptical colleagues. They may be right and I may be wrong. I don't know. But in my uncertainty, when I had to risk error, I preferred to err, as my friend Scott Sullivan likes to say, on the side of humanity.

John Dewey said that "the inclination to learn from life itself and to make the conditions of life such that all will learn in the process of living is the finest product of schooling" (1966, 51). My experience in the classroom after the death of Steve has me believing that I need to work harder still to find ways to connect "life itself" with life in school; in fact, to try to make the two, insofar as it's possible, one. The world, after all, is actually a much better classroom than a classroom. But the artificial distinction between the two is, of course, a necessity. We can't all be wandering about the planet with our 125 students gathered around us. So I want my classroom to be one that is ready to receive the world when it decides to come crashing through the windows, as it did that Monday morning.

But in order to bring together "life itself" and schooling, I think I have to know my kids, know Kids, know their interests, their prejudices, their ways of facing challenge and adversity, their ways of showing pleasure, disdain, interest, and anger, and their ways of disguising these feelings; I want to learn how to better "read" what the kids choose to reveal to me. I think that is essential, not only because it's humane, but because it makes good pedagogical sense. If one of my aims is to connect new material with existing knowledge and beliefs, perhaps I need to aspire to know my kids at least as well as I know my subject matter.

Sometimes I like to think that my students know very well how to ask for what they need and are teaching me how to listen. They are ingenious at finding ways to reveal themselves to their teachers. They sulk, they disengage, they argue if the work we give them seems meaningless. They work overtime, share their excitement with family and friends, want to talk about what they've done when they feel the work is consequential.

I have scattered elsewhere throughout this book letters, notes, and comments I received from students who were displeased with the way I conducted my class. "Part III: Conversations with Students" offers a sampling of some of the letters I received from students for whom my efforts seemed to pay off. These writings are part of our attempts to know each other and ourselves as teachers, as students, as people so we can better teach and learn from one another, even while we and our world continue to change.

# Chapter Seven

# Put It In Writing

*I have found one of the most valuable qualities a teacher can have is the ability to perceive and build upon the needs his pupils struggle to articulate through their every reaction. For this he needs antennae and must constantly work upon attuning himself to the ambiance of the classroom.*

Herbert Kohl

Just as a French teacher might insist that her students always speak French in her room even if they are asking permission to leave it momentarily, I ask my students to put most of their requests, complaints, suggestions, and thoughts into writing. As often as possible, I reply in writing.

Here are pieces of notes and letters I received from the kids. Some writings were formal, some hastily scribbled on notebook paper and left on my desk, others were year's-end reflections that accompanied students' final-grade proposals. I offer these with the hope that it will help us look through the kids' eyes, see how all of this—the reading and writing workshops, the portfolios, the self-assessment, the experimentation—appears to them.

### Writing

While looking through the pile of this year's essays, I found a big difference—and a *real* difference between the stuff I have written recently and stuff I wrote last fall. The difference is an urgency in the writing. The urgency is there because there is something I need to say. There is something I need to say because I am not writing an essay just for English class, but because I am telling you "where the book hit me"—as you like to say.

I am writing this way because you have shown me that it is valid, and you relaxed while I tried it out. Before, my real response to books was something completely separate from English class and English essays. I wrote English essays because I was supposed to. You can tell. They plod. They are stiff. They kind of gawk away from the subject matter. The essays I wrote this year, the latter ones, may or may not be better written, but they pull me through the paper with their urgency. I much prefer to write out of urgency.

Natasha Saleski


I thrived on the creative writing we got to do each quarter. We wrote and rewrote papers until they got accepted (man, I lived for that COMPLETED stamp—each stamp meant my portfolio was that much thicker). You always gave us this advice: "Write what you care about." This concept seems so simple now, but to a group of students that had grown up in Five-Paragraph-Essayland, it made a huge difference. And by telling each and every student, whatever their ability level, to write what they care about, you were saying that you would not have prejudged notions about what this guy [I've been reading in college] Bordeieu calls "cultural capital." You seemed to be saying to each student, "I see you all as having equal cultural capital. You can write passionately on subjects that you enjoy or on aspects of your own life. I will not judge your language codes, and I will not judge the topics you've chosen." This allowed every student to see herself as a writer and to find her own voice.

You did have guidelines for us. Ahh, the big three: Clarity, Insight, and Evidence. We couldn't just rattle off a piece of crap filled with run-ons and mechanical errors. But instead of giving us a big fat D and moving on to the next paper, you pushed and prodded and cajoled and begged for rewrite after revision after revision after revision. And we delivered. I wrote some of my favorite stuff in your class. You have, possibly without even knowing it, defied the norms of the educational system and invited students to evaluate their own worth.

Louisa Kaplan

Thanks to you, I like to write poems. When you and me sat that time and you read me my poem, you was the first person to understand them. Before I was afraid to let people read what I wrote because they wouldn't understand it. Ever since you understood my poems, I sent them into this contest and became a semi-finalist. Now I let every body read my poems, I don't care if they understand or not. Every chance I get, I always write down what ever is on my mind. I want you to know I will continue to write.

Andrea Foster

Before I leave ETHS, I have to thank you for what you gave me nearly four years ago. I [recently came across] my freshman portfolio. I opened it up and inside were my works that I'd totally forgotten. As I reread them, it occurred to me that my interest in writing had almost been a fluke! I remembered how I ventured into a sarcastic, funny style and turned in a bold satire for a portfolio entry just because I didn't have anything else at the time.

Mr. Larson, you loved it! I got it back and loved reading your comments and decided to try it again. Each time I turned something in you were excited and caught up in the whole experience of my work. Basically, you gave me the invaluable gift of confidence in my writing. This feeling has stuck with me throughout high school.

Jon Seyfried

The next letters are from students, all of whom were, in my estimation, very bright, intuitive, and articulate kids; both of whom also possessed language difficulties. The first, Gretchen, has a pronounced learning disability; the second, Paulo, is still struggling to learn English. He had recently arrived from Brazil.[1] Both of these

---

[1]Paulo is one of the students Anny referred to in her letter in Chapter 4 about students with language deficiencies.

students' writing obstacles were complex. I could not possibly solve these problems in my nine months as their teacher. I had to make decisions about what I would work with and what I would leave to subsequent teachers.

Try to see past Gretchen's peculiar spellings and see through to her desire to educate teachers and fellow students about what it is like to have an LD. And as you read Paulo's letter, try to see past his unusual syntax and see through to his excitement about writing stories. First, Gretchen:

> I have gathered here what I beleive to be my strongest pices of writting. Not only are they strong in the littiary sence, but they are powerful expressions of my feeling as a writter and as an individual. I struggel with the process of writing. I always have wondeful thought although the germatice, punquation and other esential pices of writting don't alway work out the best whem I'm writting. Because of my learning disablity I often run into prolems that can only be concered wityh the assistance of a nother person.
>
> I have chosen to include [in my portfolio] a pice intitaled "Living With a Learning Disability" I chose to include this pice because I put a lot of time and care into writting it and it exsplains in great detail who I am as a writter. I feal it was important for me to write it because it allowed me to relize who I was as a student and it would be very benificial to others who wonted to understand me as a student.
>
> Gretchen Burns

From Paulo:

> On this school year I had learned many different things. I had learn how to use a quadratic equation and I had learn that an iceberg contains more heat than a cup of water. But one of the things I had learn the most are my writing ability. These year I had focus in writing more than I ever did before. I had found writing fun, and I get excited every time that I sit down and start to imagine places that only exist on my mind. The pen has become one of my most important tools because it links these two worlds. A pen meets my imagination and translates

my thoughts into reality. My story grows with each day that passes, and as well for my passion of writing.

Paulo

Writing for me is like an answer to any problem, or bad feeling that I may have. It aids me in relieving stress, and if I didn't discover my talent for writing then my past would be nothing but trouble. Writing clears the evil thoughts in my mind. Writing also helps me tell people of the good things in life. The cure for my blues is simply pen and paper.

Raquel Mathews

Becky Weiss, a senior in my AP class, took five AP tests and received the highest marks on all of them. She is now attending Harvard University. One of the things I admired most about Becky, however, was her decision to take a risk this year and write "something meaningful." She had lamented to me on numerous occasions that although she was a straight-A student, she had never written anything that meant anything to her. Here is part of her year's-end reflection:

Becky the writer has much more to learn than Becky the reader. At the beginning of the year, I had never written anything that I found particularly meaningful. However, I was determined that this year I would produce a work that was an expression of me. [I wrote] a poem called "A Place Filled With Joy" which has undergone many revisions, and although I am satisfied with it insofar as it conveys what I wanted it to convey, I realize that it is far from perfect. Nevertheless, it is the first meaningful writing I have ever done, and it therefore represents great improvement in this area.

Rebecca Weiss

I cannot put my finger on what you did to make writing so important to me. I am confident that it was a combination of things: your enthusiasm, your time put into reading each work, your helpful encouraging comments in the margins of every page. Whatever it was, it worked. You created an environment in which it was safe to experiment with writing, to force the horizons of the mind to expand. I enthusiastically discarded my previous notions of how writing should be organized and I plunged into a more sophisticated and thought-provoking style.

Maggie Beeler

## Reading

Reading is probably the most personal of all the facets of English class. We can be guided to look for certain things in a book, or an intended message, but no one can dictate our mood when we read, no one can dictate what we think when we are reading.

I am a very slow reader—I often have a hard time picking everything up on the first pass. But the freedom, or better yet, the lack of dictation of how far we need to be by a specific point in time has done wonders for me as a reader. The fact that I wouldn't have to worry about a quiz or essay every week made me much more comfortable taking my time with the reading, indulging myself in the reading almost.

Peter Seagall

This year you gave us a whole different style of learning, with this new free reading you gave us a choice of the reading that we want to read, instead of the (old) everyone reads the same book at the same pace and most of the time reading the old way people skip pages just to get where the fast readers are at. I like this reading because it lets everyone read at their own pace.

Steven Terrell

I learned how to find myself in a book.

Rafael Altamirano

Before taking your class, I wasn't much of a reader because I didn't even really know what types of books I enjoyed reading. You told our class to find a book that we would enjoy and find it easy to talk about. For me that was a problem. At first I chose one book but just couldn't get into it. I told you the problem I was having and you told me that I was wasting my time if the book had no meaning for me. Then I picked *Kitchen God's Wife* by Amy Tan. I found out how much I really enjoyed books that talk about families and their cultures.

Claire Nelson

I learned that becoming part of what you read makes it easier to understand and stay interested.

Steve Barnes

Last year was the ten-year anniversary of my mother's death. It was an extremely painful time in my life and I am never totally comfortable with the event. In three books we read, *As I Lay Dying*, *The Death of Ivan Illych*, and *Night*, I saw myself and my painful memories. In the essays I wrote on those books, I expressed my inner thoughts on my mother's death and its connection to the stories. As I reread the essays recently, I was mesmerized by the emotions they provoked in me. After those writings, and others like them, I finally felt at peace with my mom and her death.

Ari Studnitzer

I will never forget this: It was one of those days when I was just a wreck, and I realized when I got to English that it was the day that I was scheduled to have my final grade conference. Great, just what I needed. So I went up to talk to you, and we started talking about *Native Son*, the book we had just finished reading. I told you how much I loved that book and why, and you got up out of your chair. You went to your bookcase and got a copy of Wright's *The Outsider*. You told me to keep it—said that if I liked *Native Son* this might interest me. I don't think I can tell you how much that meant to me. You might not even remember it, but it touched me deeply.

L. S.

## Learning

Whenever the students have a major research paper to do, I write one of my own. I keep to the same assignment parameters and deadlines as they do. I want to be like a coach who will "run the mile" with his team. I believe this gives students important opportunities to watch as an adult works through some of the same processes and problems they are facing. I experience many of the same emotions they do: excitement at first, then bewilderment, later stress, and finally relief and pride. It seems to give them comfort. My writing a paper also helps students take the project seriously, as if it were a real-world challenge and not a manufactured task for school, one that I as an adult wouldn't dream of doing now that I'm "finished" with my education.

One year, I wrote a paper on learning and focused on a reflection on my own education. I later received a lengthy letter from a senior who, just as she was about to graduate, took a long, hard look at her own education. Here is part of that letter:

> Your research paper has reminded me to think about education as it applies to me specifically. This is something that I have been trying to do more of this year, but as I continually fail to come to any conclusions, it scares me to keep thinking. I know that I will go to school, that I have always gone to school, and that I will continue to go to school. I know that I remember begging my mother to call the principal to ask him to open the school on weekends. I know I like school now; I memorize, I read, and I think that I am learning, but I am not sure. In classes like French I can feel my head becoming fuller. I can communicate with people in French. I am fairly sure this is learning. I also know a lot about biology. God, I have learned a lot of facts in that class. (I only wish they made me a better person.)
>
> I would like to understand what gave me the drive to do well in school. Was it a basic instinct that told me that if I was going to work at something I might as well work to achieve the highest level possible? Was it something my father said to me after I failed my first test, or was it an accumulation of events? If it was something my parents said, that scares me because I might not be able to say the right things to my children.
>
> I think that most people like knowing stuff, relating stuff. I know that I do. I remember that one of the first things that

impressed me about you was the way one thing was constantly reminding you of another. You were able to read a piece of writing and pull up some conversation you had, some movie you'd seen. The feeling of possessing knowledge is definitely one thing that makes me want to learn. I like knowing the answer to Final Jeopardy. I like understanding what I read. I also like talking to people about ideas. Sure I like these things and they make me happy, but sometimes I wonder if they are enough. Maybe that's what being educated is, but maybe one has to apply and share knowledge for it to be worth anything at all. I just don't know.

I am not sure if I can trace the relationship between what you have written and this set of observations, but hopefully this letter has been of some interest to you. I know it has made me feel good to write it.

Karen Van Ausdal

I responded to Karen's letter:

"Knowing stuff" *is* fun. It provides many rewards: praise from our elders, good grades, the admiration of our peers, and personal satisfaction. It's also useful, of course. But what really interested me in what you wrote, what really showed me the level of your intelligence and maturity, was your leap of faith in seriously asking, perhaps for the first time, if "knowing stuff is enough."

It's always been my belief that intelligence is not so much a matter of how much stuff one knows as it is her ability to make connections between the things she knows and to make something with it: a computer, a rocket, a theorem, a serum, a concept, an opera, Velcro. . . .

You ask what makes you stretch yourself. Are you looking for a single factor? Obviously not. It is partly your parents, both before and after the womb, partly your community, your school, friends, your own intelligence, temperament. . . . The list is long. Will you pass it on to your children? That, I think, is inescapable. Some of it you will make a conscious effort to pass on. Much of it you will convey without thinking. It's already stored in who you are. I like what Einstein said: "The only rational way of educating is to be an example." Keeping that in mind keeps me alert. I have to be aware of the example I set. I don't want students to accidentally learn something I don't want to teach them—like hating to read or to be bored with ideas, or to value answers more than questions, or to lose patience with ambiguity.

Lastly, I was fascinated by your evaluation of your own education here at ETHS. You know how to perform well, you're smart, you enjoy challenges, and you "followed the pattern." School has served you well. And even so, you raise questions, in these final moments of your high school career, about what you learned. "I guess I must be learning," you say, though quizzically. Reading between the lines, I think I can see that you are beginning to realize that real learning is not nearly as recognizable nor easily measurable as we once thought, or would like to continue to think. Your observations and questions are valuable to you and to me, and to other educators, too, who like to wonder, "How else might this be done?"

This is a letter from a senior, Dan Ring, who wrote that "On the first day of class when you told us there would be no grades, you said, "Some of you will probably have a hard time dealing with this." Almost everyone lied and said they wouldn't; well, I know I did. It took me a full three months to deal with it, yet at the same time I was cognizant of the fact that I was freer than I ever had been in school before. Dan said that for the first time he made a conscious effort "not to play it safe," and added: "Every point I brought up in class, I believed, and everything that I soaked up from others in our discussions I tried to integrate into my papers, not because it was "correct" or because there was a list of answers to questions that needed to be there, but because I only had one prerequisite for myself: Be true."

He ended his letter with this metaphor:

In the middle of your classroom, there's this rectangular patch of carpeting that's missing. When I noticed it a few months ago, it took me back to when I was seven years old and in my first synagogue.

The rabbi at that time was a warm man with a wry sense of humor. He would tell jokes about the bima and wink at you at the craziest times. One day our class had occasion to visit him in his office and one of us noticed that a panel of his ceiling was missing. When we inquired about when he would repair it, he responded that it was supposed to be that way. Why, we asked. He said it reminded him that no matter how old he was or how much he knew about Judaism and the Torah, there is still more to learn. Just as the ceiling will be incomplete, the minds of men will never contain every bit of knowledge in the world. I thought that was just so beautiful.

Mr. Larson, that bit of missing carpet in your room reminds me that there will always be new things to learn, and new ways to learn them.

I had several students both as freshmen and later as seniors. It was always interesting to see the difference in them, to see how much they had grown, physically, emotionally, and academically. And they were aware of the changes in me too. Here is a letter from one such student who knew me the year before I eliminated grades and began working with portfolios. She returned to my classroom as a senior.

I got to thinking about when you knew me as a freshman, and how different things were then. When I was a freshman in your class, I was, well, terrified. The whole idea of high school was scary, and it was made even worse when I was dealing with teachers. The teachers in high school were different from the ones in grade school—more . . . real, I guess. You were the most real of all. You had stories to tell, a life of your own, an interest in things not involved with the high school. Basically, you were cool.

But there was one major way you were the same as other teachers. Grading. And that, unfortunately, sometimes canceled out everything else that made you cool. You gave us the same homework, the same tests, the same rules, and it always came down to the number of points in the grade book—no questions asked. I'll admit that there was many a time when I would sit in my room the night before a test and cry. I knew damn well I wasn't going to get away with anything on one of your killer tests.

Then I had you again as a senior, but things were different this time—and, if you can believe it, at least as scary as before. All of a sudden you wanted me to do something that I had never been asked to do—honestly assess myself. Also, you took away all the tests and quizzes—and took with them a tangible way of assessment. But, somehow, with an endless amount of patience, you coached me through it. At our first grade conference, I sat across from you, clutching a pile of poems I had written and a few book critiques. You asked me questions about my goals, something no one had ever done before . . . and you really cared about the answers. You talked to me as if I were a person, and not just a senior in your many English classes. I was an adult—I was your friend. Because of this, I was able to find a motivation inside myself; not because I had to, but because I wanted to. You helped me find something in me that I never knew existed. Thank you so much.

Liz Schaffer

# Chapter Eight

# First and Last Day Letters

At the beginning of the year, I ask my students to write an essay exploring what they think English class is for. Most kids tend to play it safe so early in our relationship, sticking with standard responses: "English class is to broaden our horizons" and "To read great works of the past." Some are more brazen, letting me know from the start that they're cynics: "For a grade, what else?" Few students, however, consider the question very deeply. Indeed, it wasn't until recently that even I, an English teacher, asked myself what English class is for. Try it sometime. It's a deceptively simple question, like Studs Terkel's, "Who are you?" but one worth revisiting each year both on our own and with our colleagues. Here's the response I wrote to the class of 1997:

> David Denby, in his book, *Great Books*, writes about a Columbia University literature professor who started his class one year by saying, "You're here for very selfish reasons. You're here to build a self. You create a self, you don't inherit it" (31).
>
> You're here to build a self. I liked that. But how is it done?
>
> I've heard it said that you are the sum of all your experiences, great and small. With each encounter you have with a person, group of people, book, movie, or even yourself, you are assembling, creating your *self*. We're all our own Dr. Frankensteins, perhaps, crafting a new "creature" out of scraps

of this and that. And that's where education comes in, I believe. While you are building your self, education exposes you to possibilities of high quality.

The sixties used an interesting phrase: "You are what you eat." I never really knew what that meant. But then I read that Plato believed that you become what you read, and suddenly that odd phrase from long ago made sense to me. Today we might say that you are what you watch, what you listen to, as well as what you read. School, I think, has a responsibility to feed you well as you build, as you create.

If you don't read and read widely, if you remain uninformed of what is happening in the world, if you don't know what early as well as contemporary authors have to say, you remain a prisoner of your own limitations. Your thinking will not, cannot advance.

If you have any doubt about the importance of education and reading and writing, look at any oppressive society. Hitler, for example, burned books. American slave owners outlawed teaching slaves to read. In his autobiography, Frederick Douglass writes about how his master's wife taught him to read the Bible so he could "be closer to God." When her husband found out, he exploded, "It will unfit him to be a slave!"

Yes! That's just the point! As Bill Ayers says, "Education will unfit anyone to be a slave. That is because education is bold, adventurous, creative, vivid, illuminating—in other words, education is for self-activating explorers of life, for those who would challenge fate, for doers and activists, for citizens" (1993, 138). Education will fill you with the power of possibility, it will open worlds, it will teach you to think and to argue, to read well, to write with conviction and grace, to stand up when you must and say with the power of assurance, "This is not right"—and with that, the possibility of changing the world. Books and writing are that powerful.

Everything we will do here in English class is meant to take you one step closer to being able to look at the world for yourself and to make up your own mind—*in an informed and reasoned way*—about what you see and hear. English class exposes you to different viewpoints and possibilities, and when it works as it should, it equips you with the skills of analysis, argumentation and reflection necessary to making your way

through the world living up to your highest potential.
You are here to build a self.
Make it a good one.

I wrote the following letter to my students at the end of one particularly difficult year. Many students had taken on huge projects for the fourth quarter and found that the projects grew as they worked on them. Some were discouraged because they didn't finish or because the end-product didn't live up to their expectations. I have since given this letter to other classes on the last day of school.

My parting wish for you is that you learn—or recognize that you have learned—to be both subjective about and appreciative of your own efforts and to establish a set of standards that mean something to you—standards that you are willing to constantly, fearlessly reevaluate. I've come to believe that we must arrive at some personal definition of success if we are going to be happy—if, in fact, we are to be successful. Too much time and energy can be lost aspiring to someone else's notion of success.

Completing tasks "successfully" is largely how school measures success. It's probably what you are most used to. But it's not the only way to succeed. Are the people who strive daily to find a cure for AIDS failures because their work is not yet finished, may not be finished for years? I don't see it that way. The documentation of their efforts, of their failures as well as their successes, is extremely important to what one of you once called "the great wad of information."

Remember when Randall P. McMurphy in *One Flew Over the Cuckoo's Nest* tries, on a bet, to lift a huge and impossibly heavy panel? He fails, but as he walks out of the room, he says to the assembly of chuckling inmates, "I tried though. I sure as hell did that much, now, didn't I?" In the end it is his effort that matters. (It was a bogus task anyway.) In that assembly is McMurphy's friend, Chief Bromden, who is witness not to McMurphy's failure but his *effort*. Inspired by what he had seen, Bromden later manages to lift the panel himself and it literally sets him free. I have admiration for people who try big things and have the courage to face failure.

Am I a failure because, though I tried very hard, I didn't succeed in everything I set out to accomplish in the classroom this year? I don't see it that way. Of course, I have pangs when I think of what I did not accomplish. But these pangs spark my future efforts. I think of what I once heard Elie Wiesel say about the characters and incidents that he ultimately had to leave out of his books. They cry out in the night, he said. Those goals I didn't attain and those students for whom I wasn't successful *do cry* out in the night. But I'm not a failure, I believe, until I stop listening, stop trying. I'm not a failure if I take the time to think about why I failed and to make the necessary adjustments—and try again.

Are you a failure in this class because, though you tried very hard, you may not have finished every book or every task or achieved every goal you set for yourself? I don't see it that way. Not if your effort was genuine and you've given a generous amount of time to looking closely, very very closely at what you learned in the process. We're works-in-progress, that's something that will never change.

I have great admiration for those of you who grappled with huge projects this year because you wanted to test your wingspan or because you found, as you worked, that the project grew beyond your expectations; I admire those of you who tangled with the extremely difficult task of taking a hand in your own education and articulating what you want from it; my hat is off to those of you who found ways to push *yourselves* and those of you who were willing to step into the chaos in an effort to create order. I admire and cherish the letters and notes I received from so many of you. They tell me that you were willing to begin to take the reins into your own hands where they belong. Are you finished? Not by a long shot. But you've come so very far.

And lastly, I'm grateful to those of you who challenged my thinking and me, face to face and on paper. You forced me daily to turn inward and ask myself if what I was doing was right, was fair, was working, was valid, was successful. You reminded me to think of my own definition of success as a work-in-progress. The result is a highly personalized notion of achievement that I'm learning to adjust. It remains vital because it's mine and it grows with me. I simply couldn't have done this without you.

If you have not done so already, I urge you to give some

serious thought to your own definition of success, now, today. Put it in writing. And remember that it's a draft. If you don't, you may be tempted to let others define it for you or to adapt some prepackaged notion. And that won't do. The victories will be hollow and lack resonance and longevity. Look to what has meaning for you. Ralph Waldo Emerson said it this way:

> To laugh often and much; to win the respect of intelligent people and affection of children; to earn the appreciation of honest critics and endure the betrayal of false friends; to appreciate beauty, to find the best in others; to leave the world a bit better, whether by a healthy child, a garden patch, or a redeemed social condition; to know even one life has breathed easier because you have lived. This is to have succeeded.

However you define it—however *you* define it—I wish you success.

Farewell.

# Afterword

# As the Best We Know How to Be

*Our story never ends with a neat conclusion, our data is mostly unruly and insufficient, and our jigsaw puzzle is always incomplete because it is always fluid, always changing. Whatever truths we discover are contingent; our facts are tentative. This is because we are interested in children—living, breathing, squirming, growing, moving, messy, idiosyncratic children. Just when we have gained some worthwhile insight, just when we have captured some interesting essence, the children change, the kaleidoscope turns, and we must look again, even more deeply.*

William Ayers

I stood at my mailbox, pitching most of its contents straight into the nearby recycling box. A colleague pressed his palm to the small of my back and joked, "No missives from Mark, today?"

"I've got one coming soon," I said, as always a bit too earnestly.

My friend laughed. "Why do you sweat this so much? You work too hard. Relax. Unset your jaw."

Why do I sweat this? Why do I work so hard? For the sake of the children! Their physical and emotional lives are at stake. *Blah, blah, blah.* I'd said it all before, and though I do believe it on one level, the words sounded particularly hollow today.

My colleague laughed again and said, "Down, boy, down."

I won't lie to you. So far, engaging in this conversation with colleagues has not been easy. Yes, there are Susan and Fred and Anny; Theresa and Warren; Larry, Val, Carol, Syd, Hilda; and many, many others who question themselves and the school openly and with rel-

ish. But many teachers, for reasons of their own, resist any conversation at all. Some say, "I'm too close to retirement." Some say,
"What I'm doing has worked for me for years." Some say, "Been
there, done that." Some say, "I just don't have time." Some have
called me "arrogant," "self-aggrandizing," and "whining." But most
teachers respond to our letters and invitations with silence. That's
the worst.

The gap between those of us who wish to challenge the way
things are and our more acquiescent colleagues, whatever its caus-
es—their seeming resistance, our supposed arrogance, or both—cannot be permitted to widen. Vaclav Havel warned against getting "too
far ahead of the pack [. . .] The risk," he said, "can far outweigh the
actual significance of the good intentions. Moreover, one can easily
lose touch with the group, and thus lose the chance of positively
influencing it as well." We must exercise (or cultivate) "the sensitivity to judge whether we are about to make that inspiring step forward, or are, through a display of bravado, toying with fate and thus
arousing only resistance in our partners" (1992, 100).

This resistance has taken many forms and has many sources. I
have displayed my share of acts of bravado, bluntly challenging
methods and tests in which many teachers have great and long-last-
ing faith. I imagine, too, that at times I do appear arrogant. I've been
told that I sometimes sound as though I have all the answers. That's
unfortunate and not at all what I intend. I once put off my colleagues
by referring in a letter to "an educational expert." I wouldn't hesitate
to cite a source again—isn't that what we English teachers always
tell our kids to do?—but I will be more aware of and sensitive to the
very real skepticism some teachers feel toward theorists. It is skepticism that has long been in place and often for good reason.
Nothing, however, has been more tricky than finding ways to question the way things are without sounding as though we are criticiz-
ing teachers who have devoted their entire careers to those ways of
teaching.

When I was thirty, I had a sixty-year-old friend who was an
entertainer. We were having dinner one night, and I was raving
about a new Lena Horne double album I had just bought. He listened
but grew visibly upset. Finally, he snapped, "You act like you discovered Lena Horne!" Here I was, half his age, telling *him* about
Lena Horne. The incident came back to me recently while I was
reading, for the first time, the work of John Dewey. Because of my

previous experience, I was hesitant to rave too loudly in front of my older colleagues. However, I've begun to wonder whether, in a very real sense, I did discover John Dewey and I did discover Lena Horne. I was going to say *re*discover, but I do mean discover. Perhaps each generation discovers the past for itself and in its own way. The world will have changed, so the context will have changed. I will read Dewey in a way that necessarily will be different from the way my colleagues had read him.

But I hope that as we discuss method, curriculum, and philosophy, we will strive to embrace the advice of experienced teachers, some of whose careers have spanned three decades of change. What they must have to offer! And they *are* right. There's little that we have to say that is new. Much of what we are trying today—from block scheduling to alternative forms of assessment—has already been tried by them. The most significant differences are in what we've learned about learning in the interim and the context, the world, in which these methods and ideas are being tested. The kaleidoscope will have turned. But "nothing's lost forever," Harper, a character in Tony Kushner's *Angels in America* assures us. "In this world, there is a kind of painful progress. Longing for what we've left behind, and dreaming ahead."

## Dreaming Ahead

I am writing the very end of this book in the summer. I have the leisure to close my eyes from time to time and dream ahead to the day in September when I will return to my classroom and a new group of students.

It won't be the classroom I left. I have a new one. They moved me again. And I know I won't be the same teacher who left last June, either. I envision myself still giving students a lot of say in how we fashion their education, but I will also seek more efficient ways to guide and inform that conversation. I will give my students choice in what they read and how we'll approach those works, and I will talk them through the difficult and confusing matter of how to make their choices. I will look for ways to draw students toward works from the canon, but also strive for an annual reassessment of that list, a conversation that will include students.

I will continue to struggle toward ways to help students discover their own voices when they write, then seek out ways to assist them in honing what they have written. And I will continue to look for ways to help them assess their own work and progress in meaningful ways.

I'll also be trying to find ways to become more comfortable with my role as teacher: part authoritarian and part member of the group; part learner and part learned. As I look back over the letters compiled here, I think that I probably auditioned each of these roles separately. So I look forward to returning to my classroom in September and the chance to get better at putting together these two: teacher and learner.

## To Be a Very Good Teacher

Several months after my colleague bid me unset my jaw, I attended an assessment conference. There I heard Grant Wiggins declare that one of the most powerful motivators there is is "the desire to get better at something you value." And that made perfect sense to me. I wish I'd had that answer ready when my friend told me to relax. I "sweat it" because I want to become better at teaching, and I find that effort enormously gratifying—in fact, that "work" can actually be relaxing. The reading, the thinking, the talking that my friend might consider labor, I consider recreation. I'd rather read Paulo Freire's work poolside than John Grisham's because it's more stimulating. Practicing a golf swing or a swan dive would be drudgery for me because becoming a better golfer or diver means very little to me. I work hard at teaching because I value it. Simple as that. I want to become a very good teacher one day. But I can't do that alone.

The one thing I fear most—whether through careless disregard for the ideas of others or foolish displays of bravado—is that all of the questioning, the letters, and the ardent appeals for conversation could result, ironically, in my isolation. I fear alienating myself to the point where I'm back where I started: alone in my room.

And that won't do. "The aim," according to Maxine Greene, "is to find (or create) an authentic public space [. . .] one in which diverse human beings can appear before one another as to quote Hannah Arendt, 'the best they know how to be.' I want to cultivate, in the full view and with the help of my colleagues, "a consciousness [. . .]" as Greene says, "of what *ought* to be, from a moral and ethical point of view, and what is in the making, what *might* be in an always open world" (1988, xi). For this, I require and will continue to insist upon an honest, probing, fearless, and ongoing exchange with my colleagues, my administrators, and my students.

# Appendix A

# First Reading Draft

*Narrative creates us at the very moment it is being created.*
Toni Morrison

TITLE _____ DATE _____

1. AUDIENCE: The audience for this piece is _____

_____

_____

2. PURPOSE: I want this piece of writing to help or make the reader ____

_____

_____

_____

3. I want the voice to sound _____

_____

_____

4. Please notice and comment on _____

_____

5. I'd like to keep working on _____

_____

COMPLETED: _____ Returned for revisions: _____

| | 6 | 5 | 4 | 3 | 2 | 1 |
|---|---|---|---|---|---|---|
| **FOCUS** | | | | | | |
| **SUPPORT** | | | | | | |
| **ORGANIZATION** | | | | | | |
| **CONVENTIONS** | | | | | | |
| **STYLE** | | | | | | |
| **INTEGRATION** | | | | | | |

*Reader's Remarks*

_____

_____

_____

_____

_____

_____

_____

_____

_____

_____

_____

_____

Error code:    **Yellow = Conventions** (sp., grammar, sentence errors)
              **Pink = Diction** (word choice)

# Appendix B

# Rewrite

*True ease in writing comes from art, not chance.*

Alexander Pope

Name _____ Period _____ Date _____

Title _____ Date _____

1. This draft is different from the previous draft(s) in these ways _____

_____

_____

_____

_____

2. I made those changes because _____

_____

_____

_____

3. Please notice or comment on _____

_____

_____

_____

COMPLETED: _____ Returned for revisions: _____

# Appendix C

# Stories That Must Be Told

*You write in order to change the world knowing perfectly well that you can't, but also knowing that literature is indispensable to the world. . . . The world changes according to the way people see it, and if you alter, even by a millimeter, the way people look at reality, then you can change it.*

James Baldwin

**TASK:**

You are a reporter. I am your editor/producer. Your assignment is to go out into your world and find a story that you feel *needs to be told.* (Examples below) Tell that story to the best of your ability in two different ways: First, objectively; second, subjectively. As your editor/producer, I will establish the guidelines and the schedule under which you will work. I also reserve the right to final say on when the work is ready for the "public" to see. That's because both of our names will be on it.

There are four primary parts to this project.

**I. The Written Proposal**                                    **Due:** _____

Your first responsibility is to write a formal proposal which convinces me that the story must be told and that you are capable of telling it well. The proposal will
   A. Briefly summarize the story and tell why you feel it needs to be told.
   B. Present me with a plan. (For example, how will you get the interviews you plan to get? Who, if anyone, will be in your group?)

**II. The First Telling: A Magazine Article**                    Due: _____

This formal paper will probably be at *least* four typed pages long. I will set no maximum number of pages. In this telling, I want you to relate, as clearly as you can, *the whole story in narrative form.* Be as detailed as you possibly can be. **Most importantly, be true to the story! Tell it without letting your own opinion show through. In another word, tell it *objectively.***

**III. The Second Telling: Your Choice**                    Due: _____

Now, I want you to tell the story again, but this time, **let your own opinion show. In another word, tell it *subjectively.*** Also, I want you to apply your unique talents and interests to this second telling of the story. Below are a few examples; however, you are not limited to these possibilities. You probably have great ideas of your own.
- video documentary (5 minutes)
- radio documentary (5 minutes)
- comic book
- series of photographs
- series of drawings
- computer presentation (HyperCard, for example)
- original musical composition
- a play
- a dramatic monologue
- a song (rap, ballad, other)
- a short story

**IV. Reflection & Grade Proposal Letter**                    Due: _____

At the end of the quarter, you will write a paper in which you reflect on the process of creating this project. (Tell its biography.) This will also serve as a grade proposal letter.

**Ideas**

Tell a story about
- what Evanston was like when an older relative or friend was younger
- someone who triumphed over adversity
- remarkable courage or success or failure or kindness
- how something important was accomplished when people worked together
- how children sometimes pay for the sins of their elders
- a mistake that could not be undone
- a case of mistaken identity
- an arrest, a crime, or an accident
- an example of injustice or one of justice
- a misunderstanding leading to a crisis or to a happy surprise

# Appendix D

# Reading Response

**PAGES READ: FROM _____ TO _____**

Name _____ Period _____

Title _____ Author _____

Quote a sentence or two that caught your attention for any reason while you read today.

_____

_____

_____

Explain why the passage had an impact on you.

_____

_____

_____

Write at least one question that the reading raised in your mind, today.

_____

_____

_____

In the space below (and on the back), please write your reaction to what you read today. What did it make you think about, wonder about, or realize? What did you particularly like or dislike?

_____

_____

# Appendix E

# Self-Evaluation

**#** _____ **Date:** _____

**Name** _____ **Period** _____

## PAST

1. What have you done well in the last two weeks?
2. What are your concerns about the work you have done during this time? Are you up-to-date?
3. What strategies for learning, reading and/or writing have you used?

## PRESENT

4. What are you working on now?

    A) Reading

    B) Writing

5. How's it going? Do you need my help?

## FUTURE

6. What is your primary objective (goal) between now and the next evaluation two weeks from now?
7. How can you help yourself reach that goal. What's first?
8. What obstacles do you see? What will you do so they don't stop you?

# Works Cited

Atwell, Nancie. 1987. *In the Middle: Writing, Reading and Learning with Adolescents*. Portsmouth: Boynton/Cook Publishers.

Ayers, William. 1993. *To Teach: The Journey of a Teacher*. New York: Teachers College Press, Columbia University.

Bair, Deirdre. 1978. *Samuel Beckett, A Biography*. New York: Harcourt, Brace, Jovanovich.

Baldwin, James. 1996. "A Talk to Teachers." In *City Kids, City Teachers*, ed. William Ayers and Patricia Ford, 219–27. New York: New Press.

Bloom, Harold. 1994. *The Western Canon: The Books and School of the Ages*. New York: Harcourt, Brace and Co.

Burke, Jim. 1996. "NCTE Standards for English."Education Week. April 3.

Delpit, Lisa. 1995. *Other People's Children: Cultural Conflict in the Classroom*. New York: The New Press.

Denby, David. 1996. *Great Books: My Adventures with Homer, Rousseau, Woolf, and Other Indestructible Writers of the Western World*. New York: Simon and Schuster.

Dewey, John. 1966. *Democracy and Education*. New York: The Free Press.

Elbow, Peter. 1986. *Embracing Contraries: Exploration in Learning and Teaching*. New York: Oxford University Press.

Elbow, Peter. 1990. *What is English?* Urbana: National Council of Teachers of English.

Edgecombe, Jason. 1995. "Evanston Township High School Report on Minority Student Achievement." Evanston, Illinois

Freire, Paulo. 1994. *Pedagogy of the Oppressed, 20th Anniversary edition*. New York: Continuum.

Fullan, Michael. 1993. *Change Forces: Probing the Depths of Educational Reform*. London: The Falmer Press.

Greene, Maxine. 1988. *The Dialectic of Freedom*. New York: Teachers College Press.

Havel, Vaclav. 1992. *Summer Meditations*. New York: Vintage Books.

Hoffman, Marvin. 1996. *Chasing Hellhounds: A Teacher Learns from His Students*. Minneapolis: Milkweed.

Holt, John. 1995. *What Do I Do Monday?* Portsmouth: Boynton/Cook Heinemann.

Horton, Myles and Paulo Friere. 1990. *We Make the Road by Walking*. ed.

Brenda Bell, John Gaventa, and John Peters. Philadelphia: Temple University Press.

Kohl, Herbert. 1988. *36 Children.* New York: Plume.

Kushner, Tony. 1994. *Angels in America, Part Two: Perestroika.* New York: Theater Communications Group, Inc.

Meier, Deborah. 1995. *The Power of Their Ideas: Lessons for America from a Small School in Harlem.* Boston: Beacon Press.

Moffett, James and Wagner, Betty Jane. 1992. *Student-Centered Language Arts, K-12, 4th Edition.* Portsmouth: Boynton/Cook.

Newkirk, Thomas. "The First Five Minutes: Setting the Agenda in a Writing Conference." Quoted in Richard Straub, "The Concept of Control in Teacher Response." CCC 47.2/May 1996.

Rodriguez, Luis J. 1996. *Always Running.* New York: Touchstone.

Romano, Tom. 1987. *Clearing the Way: Working with Teenage Writers.* Portsmouth: Heinemann.

Rose, Mike. 1989. *Lives on the Boundary.* New York: Free Press.

———. 1995. *Possible Lives: The Promise of Public Education in America.* New York: Houghton Mifflin Co.

Rosenblatt, Louise M. 1995. *Literature as Exploration, 5th edition.* New York: The Modern Language Association.

Sizer, Theodore R. 1996. *Horace's Hope: What Works for the American High School.* Boston: Houghton Mifflin Co.

———. 1992. *Horace's School: Redesigning the American High School.* Boston: Houghton Mifflin Co.

Straub, Richard. May 1996. "The Concept of Control in Teacher Response: "Defining the Varieties of 'Directive' and 'Facilitative' Commentary." *College Composition and Communication* v.46:223-251. Urbana: NCTE.

Terkel, Studs. 1992. *Race: How Blacks and Whites Think and Feel About the American Obsession.* New York: The New Press.

Wiggins, Grant. 1993. *Assessing Student Performance: Exploring the Purpose and Limits of Testing.* San Francisco: Jossey-Bass.

Zelden, Theodore. 1996. *An Intimate History of Humanity.* New York: Harper-Perennial.